MY STYLE & ME

Beauty Hacks

Fashion Tips

Style Projects

CONTENTS

BEAUTY
"Beauty is being comfortable and confident in your own skin."
- Iman

BEAUTY SECRETS

These pages offer all kinds of beauty advice, from what to eat to how to look after your skin, hair, nails and body. Packed with helpful hints, fun facts and easy craft ideas, you'll discover everything you need to know about feeling and looking great from top to toe, inside and out.

BEAUTY KNOW-HOW, facts and advice will transform you into a beauty expert.

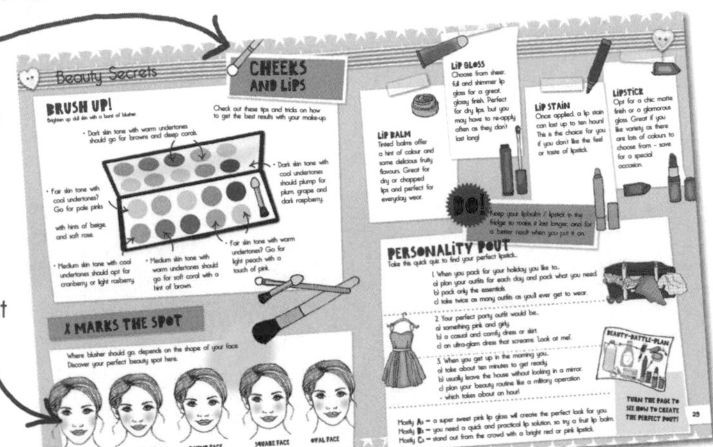

TRICKS AND TIPS will give you the confidence to try out new looks and products.

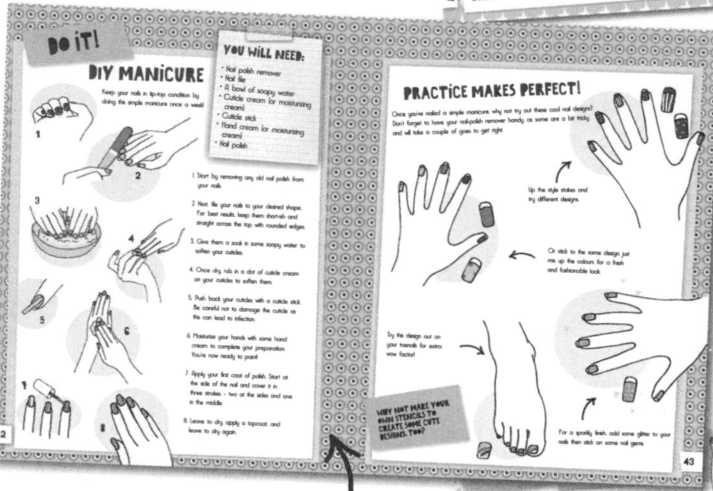

DO IT!

FOLLOW SIMPLE STEP-BY-STEP INSTRUCTIONS to make the most of your nails, skin, hair and make-up.

GET HEALTHY with fun exercises and tasty recipes to try.

MY BEAUTY ROUTINE

These pages are a chance for you to write about your beauty routine: what you like to wear, what you eat, how you look after yourself and all the make-up and style tips you've tried or would like to try.

WRITE about your month ahead here, what events you have coming up and what beauty tips and tricks you are going to try out.

DRAW or stick pictures of your favourite celebrities' and friends' looks.

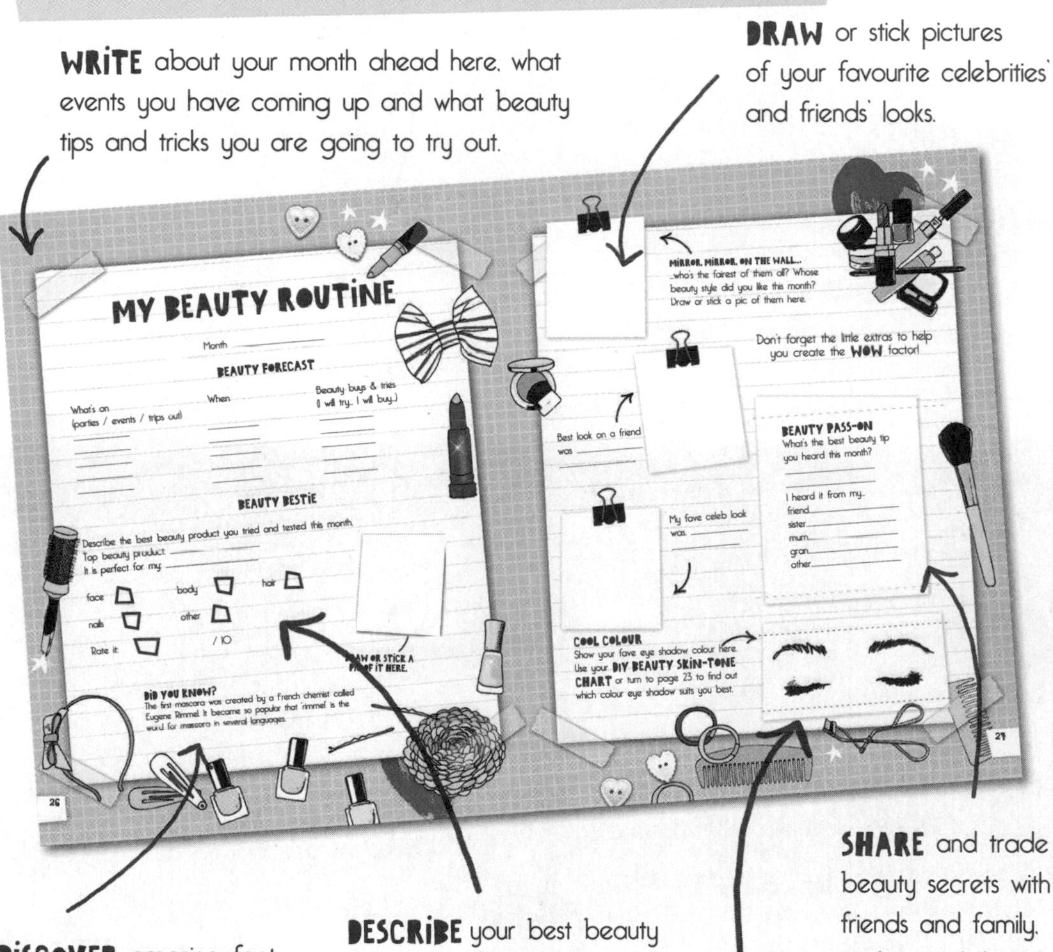

SHARE and trade beauty secrets with friends and family, and record them here.

DISCOVER amazing facts and improve your beauty know-how.

DESCRIBE your best beauty product of the month here – what you used it for and why you like it.

DOODLE and colour in the pictures to show what make-up shades and accessories suit you best.

LOVE THE SKIN YOU'RE IN

5 SIMPLE RULES OF SKINCARE

The secret to good skincare is to keep it simple...

1. **WASH** your face before you go to bed as dirt and make-up can clog your pores and irritate your skin.
2. **EXFOLIATE** your skin to remove dead skin cells and make your skin soft and smooth. To exfoliate your skin, you can use a hot flannel or a facial scrub.
3. **MOISTURIZE** your skin to stop it drying out – don't forget to wear a sunscreen on sunny days, too.
4. **EAT WELL** – take note of how your skin reacts to different foods and avoid the ones that make you blotchy!
5. Drink lots of **WATER** – dull-looking skin is often caused by dehydration. Water helps it stay soft and fresh.

BEST FOODS FOR YOUR FACE

Check out the notes below to find out what to eat and what to avoid for healthy skin.

Good...

FRUIT high in vitamin C will help your skin glow.

TOMATOES are packed with selenium, which will protect your skin from the sun.

Vitamin E found in **HAZELNUTS** will help support healthy skin growth.

Eating oily **FISH** will help keep your skin supple and stop it from looking dry.

The zinc found in **CHICKEN** will help repair damage to your skin and keep it soft.

Not so good...

Too much **BREAD** and **PASTA** can clog your pores.

Having too much **SALT** on your food can cause your skin to puff up.

Too much **SUGAR** in your diet will age your skin.

Some say **CHOCOLATE** can irritate the skin, but if you can't resist it, opt for dark chocolate.

CHIPS and other foods cooked in hot oil can make your skin look dull.

SKIN TONE

Impress your friends with some skin-tone know-how...

- Skin comes in lots of different colours. These colours, also known as skin tones, are caused by your body's supply of a pigment called melanin. People with darker skin have more melanin than people with pale skin.

- Melanin kicks in to protect your body against the sun's UV rays, and is what causes your skin to tan. People with fairer skin produce less melanin than people with darker skin, so tend to burn more easily.

- Understanding your skin tone will help you protect yourself from the sun's harmful rays and find the right shades of make-up and clothing. Use these skin-tone swatches to find the best matches for you.

SEE PAGE 55 TO FIND OUT WHAT COLOUR JEWELLERY SUITS YOUR SKIN TONE BEST.

SKIN DEEP

Your skin undertone is the colour just beneath your skin. Take this quick quiz to find out what yours is, and what looks good with it...

1. In the sun you tend to...

a) burn easily ☐

b) tan nicely ☐

2. What colour are your eyes?

a) blue, green or grey ☐

b) hazel, light brown or dark brown ☐

3. Look at the vein on the inner part of your arm. Is it...

a) more blue ☐

b) more green ☐

Mostly **As** - you're cool - you have red and pink undertones in your skin so stick to silver, grey, green and blue-red colours when choosing clothes and make-up.

Mostly **Bs** - you're warm - you have yellow, golden and peach undertones in your skin so look great in earth tones, gold, olive green and orange-red based clothing and make-up.

DO! If you want to colour your hair, make sure you pick a colour that matches your skin tone and undertone!

DO IT! DIY FACIAL

MAKE YOUR FACE GLOW WITH A DIY FACIAL!

WHAT YOU'LL NEED:

- facial cleanser
- exfoliating scrub
- washcloth
- facemask
- moisturizer

1. Clean all the dirt and make-up off your face, neck and behind your ears using a facial cleanser.

2. Use your fingers to gently rub exfoliating scrub all over your face. Use a circular motion and pay attention to oily areas like your forehead, nose and chin.

3. Fill your bowl with warm water and soak your washcloth in it. Rinse it out and press it to your face for a minute or so. Repeat two or three times.

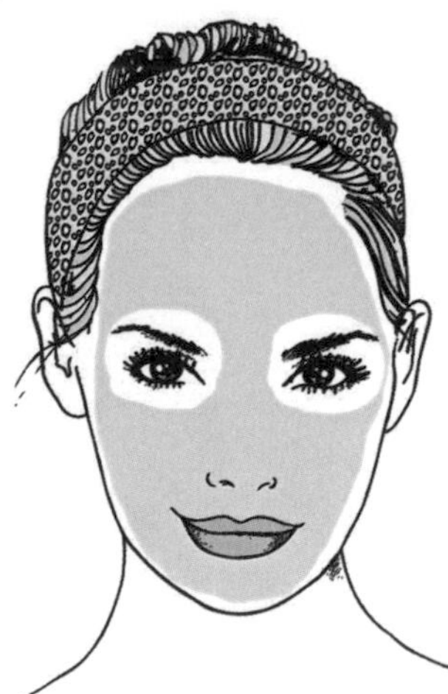

4. Apply your facemask (see opposite page for some great recipe ideas) and wash off after five to ten minutes.

5. Smooth a moisturizer over your face to finish.

WHY HAVE A FACIAL?

1. Cleansing the skin prevents skin irritation.
2. Exfoliating and removing dead skin cells from your skin will make it smoother and softer.
3. You'll feel relaxed and pampered!

Natural Beauty

MAKE YOUR OWN FACEMASKS AND CLEANSERS WITH THESE SIMPLE RECIPES...

Before applying anything to your face, always test a small amount on the back of your hand, to check it doesn't irritate your skin.

- Mash up a **BANANA** and pat it on to your face to get a great treatment for dull and flaky skin.

- Mix 1 tablespoon of **NATURAL YOGHURT** with the juice from a quarter of an **ORANGE** for a quick and easy facemask.

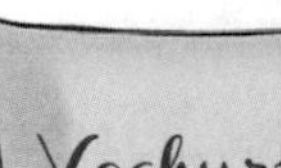

- Combine 1/2 cup of hot water with 1/3 cup of **OATMEAL** or porridge and leave for two minutes. Mix in two tablespoons of plain yoghurt, two tablespoons of honey and one egg white. Apply a thin layer of the mask to your face and leave for 15 minutes before rinsing off with warm water. This will soothe itchy skin and absorb excess oil.

- Mash up an **AVOCADO** and mix with three tablespoons of cream and one tablespoon of honey. This will create a luxurious moisturizer that will leave your skin feeling great.

- For a quick toner, mix one tablespoon of **LEMON JUICE** and two cups of water as a finishing rinse to cleanse and tighten your skin.

Make sure you don't use any ingredients you are allergic to.

MY BEAUTY ROUTINE

Month ....

BEAUTY FORECAST

What's on (parties / events / trips out)	When	Beauty buys & tries (I will try... I will buy...)
....	....	....
....	....	....
....	....	....
....	....	....
....	....	....

BEAUTY BESTIE

Describe the best beauty product you tried and tested this month.

Top beauty product: ....

It is perfect for my: ....

face ☐ body ☐ hair ☐

nails ☐ other ☐

Rate it: ☐ / 10

DRAW OR STICK A PIC OF IT HERE.

DID YOU KNOW?

Skin is the body's largest organ and makes up about 15% of your body weight.

Don't forget the little extras to help you create the WOW factor!
Get ultra stylish nails with a cool design - doodle one here.
BEAUTY PASS-ON
What's the best beauty tip you heard this month?
I heard it from my...
friend
sister
mum
gran
other
SKIN DIARY
THIS MONTH MY SKIN WAS...
normal
blotchy
greasy
dry
I ATE A LOT OF...
fruit
chocolate
crisps
vegetables
I DID THE FOLLOWING TO MY SKIN...
facial
exfoliated
moisturized
cleansed

HEALTHY HAIR

Find out how to keep your hair in tip-top condition and banish bad-hair days forever!

HAIRCARE

When it comes to having luscious locks – it's not just about what you put on your hair but what you eat too!

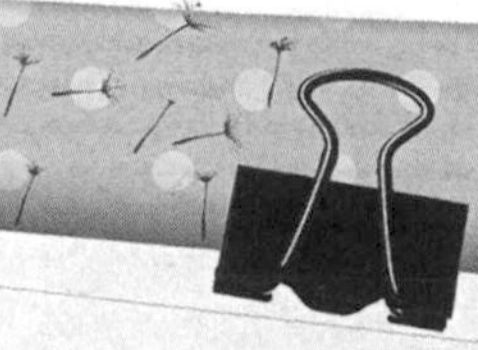

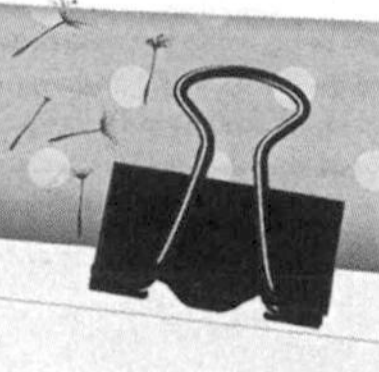

1. Biotin, an ingredient used in shampoos and conditioner to make hair shine, can also be found in **EGGS**. Time to get cracking!

2. CHICKEN and other proteins will strengthen your hair and keep your scalp healthy.

3. CHOCOHOLICS take note – vitamin B12, found in dark chocolate, will help your hair grow.

4. A **FISHY DISH** is doubly good for you as it's packed with vitamin B12 and iron, which will stop your hair falling out.

5. Superfood **SPINACH**, has a healthy dose of zinc, which will make your hair stronger and even helps prevent dandruff.

DO!

Apply your hair products at least five minutes before you style, as this gives your hair chance to absorb them, making them more effective.

CHOP CHOP!

Cutting your hair will not make it grow any faster, but cutting it every 8 to 12 weeks will make it look longer. A good cut will get rid of split ends, making your hair look thinner and shorter at the ends.

Rub wet hair with a towel after you wash it – as it will make your hair frizzy. Instead, squeeze it and leave to air-dry for a bit before you style.

WASH AND GLOW

Sometimes it's the simple things that matter in haircare... like washing it! So make sure you do it right.

1. When you cover your wet hair with shampoo, focus on the roots as this is where most dirt is.
2. Smooth the shampoo in, rather than rub or scrunch, as this will smooth the hair cuticles down.
3. After rinsing the shampoo off, apply conditioner, but this time focus on the mid-lengths and ends of the hair, as these will be the most damaged.
4. Rinse your hair with cold water before you turn off the shower. This helps seal hair cuticles and prevent frizz.

BRUSH STROKES!

Are you using the right hairbrush? Read on to find out...

A **PADDLE BRUSH** makes hair cuticles lie flat so is great for smoothing and detangling.

Use a **WIDE-TOOTHED COMB** to detangle knots in wet hair, as a bristly brush can damage it.

A **ROUND-BARREL BRUSH** is the tool of choice for blow-drying and creating bouncy curls.

The holes in a **VENT BRUSH** enable your hairdryer's heat to circulate at the roots to create more volume.

Turn the page to try out some fun and stylish hairstyles.

DO IT!

Hairstyles

Banish bad-hair days forever with these quick and nifty hairstyles.

CREATE THE PERFECT BUN

1. Select an old sock close to your hair colour and cut off the toe end to create a tube.

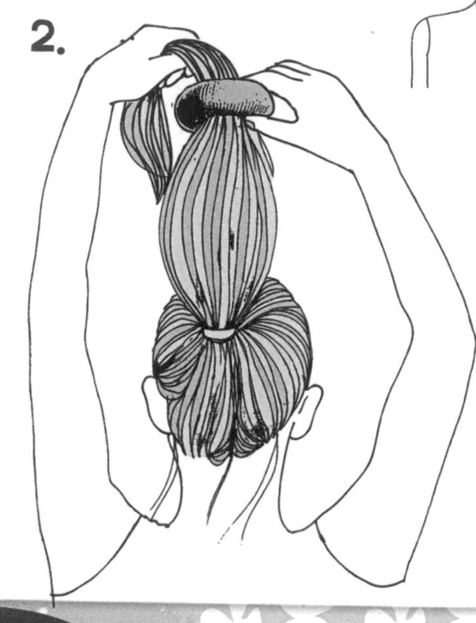

2. Put your hair in a ponytail, then roll up the sock so it's a doughnut or ring shape and pull it over the ponytail.

BEST FOR LONG HAIR!

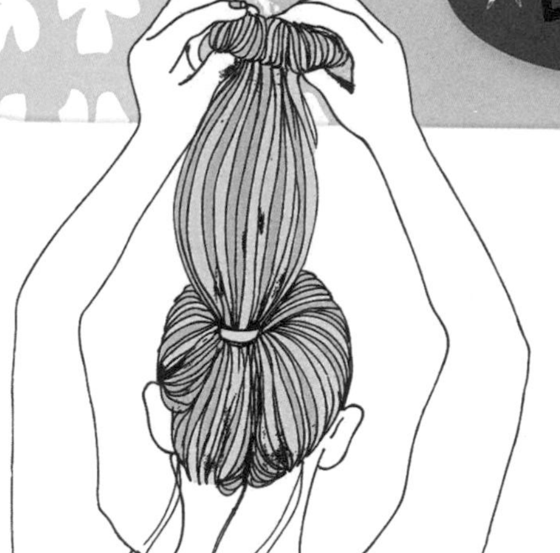

3. Pull the sock doughnut to the end of your ponytail and start to roll up your hair over it, tucking it in as you roll.

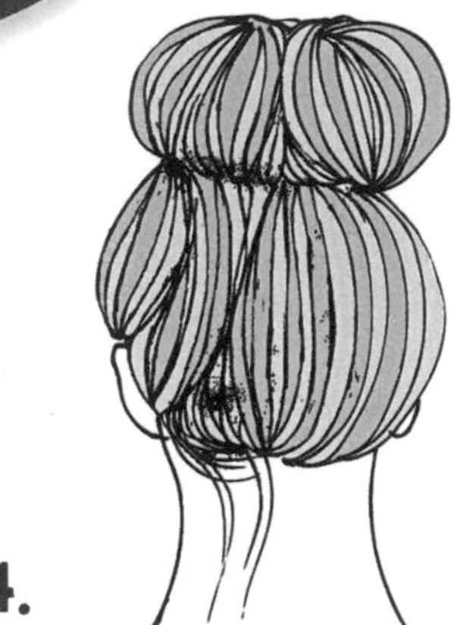

4. Slowly roll and tuck until you reach the base of your ponytail. Tidy up loose ends by pinning them around the base.

A FISHTAIL BRAID

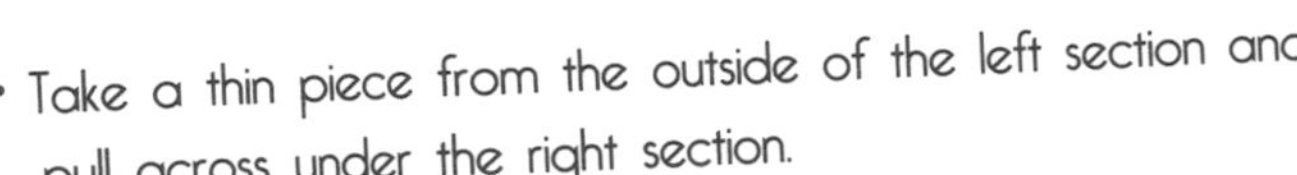

- Pull your hair into a ponytail and split into two equal sections.
- Take a thin piece from the outside of the left section and pull across under the right section.
- Take a thin piece from the outside of the right section and pull across under the left section.
- Keep going till you reach the end of your hair and secure with a hairband.

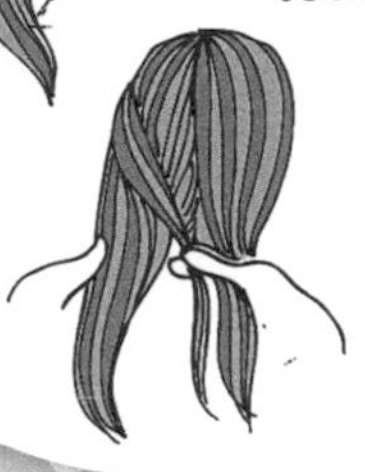

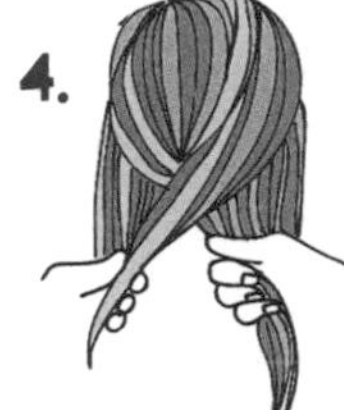

OVERNIGHT WAVES

1. After washing your hair, blow-dry it so it's 80% dry.

2. Divide into two sections and twist each section tightly, away from your face.

3. Wrap each section around itself and secure with a hairband.

4. Go to sleep, and when you wake up in the morning unravel each section, running your fingers through the waves and adding some hairspray for extra hold.

MY BEAUTY ROUTINE

Month ....

BEAUTY FORECAST

What's on (parties / events / trips out)	When	Beauty buys & tries (I will try... I will buy...)

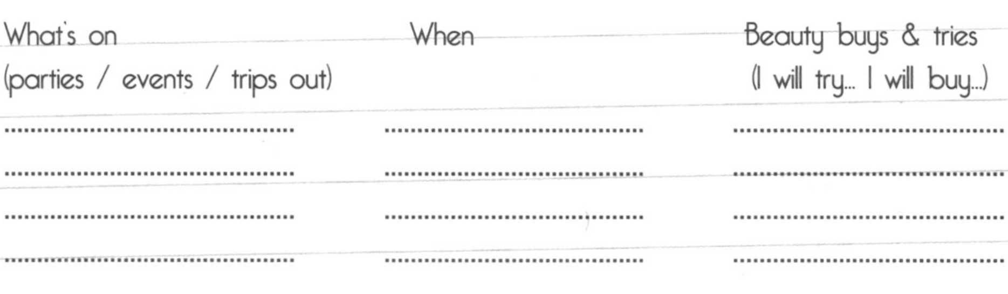

BEAUTY BESTIE

Describe the best beauty product you tried and tested this month.

Top beauty product: ....

It is perfect for my: ....

face ☐ body ☐ hair ☐

nails ☐ other ☐

Rate it: ☐ / 10

DRAW OR STICK A PIC OF IT HERE.

DID YOU KNOW?

You get goosebumps when it's cold because your hair follicles get smaller, causing your skin to bunch up and hairs to stand on end.

Don't forget the little extras to help you create the WOW factor!
Colour in these clothes to show what colours you've worn most this month.
MIRROR, MIRROR, ON THE WALL...
...who's the fairest of them all? Whose beauty style did you like this month? Draw or stick a pic of them here.
My fave celeb look was ....
Best look on a friend was ....
USE THE SPACE BELOW TO DRAW OR STICK SOME PICS OF HAIRSTYLES YOU'VE TRIED THIS MONTH, THEN RATE THEM.
Rate it: / 10
Rate it: / 10
Rate it: / 10

YOUR HAIR

Read on to discover how to make the best of your hair...

A CUT ABOVE

A good haircut can totally transform your look. Check out the face shapes below, then find your match to discover which cut will suit you best.

OVAL

Any haircut will suit your face – from bobs to pixie crops and long layered locks. Lucky you!

LONG

Widen your face with a chin-length bob or a cute fringe. Long hair will drag your face down, but if you do want it long, add some soft waves or curls.

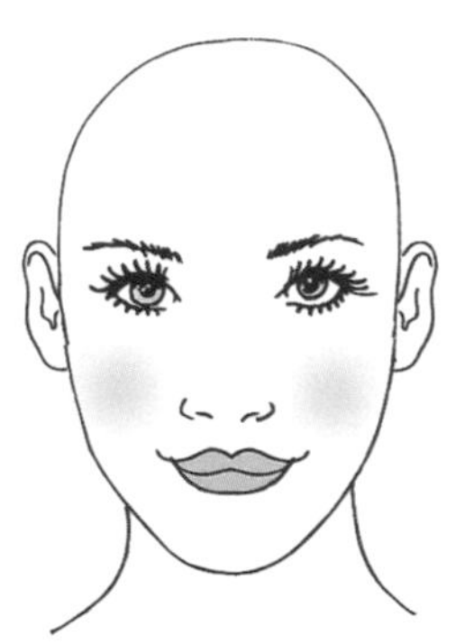

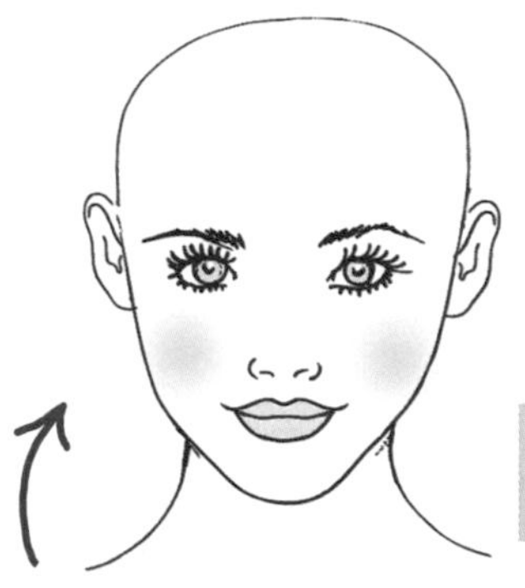

SQUARE

Try to soften your face with long layers that start just below your jawline. A side parting will help too.

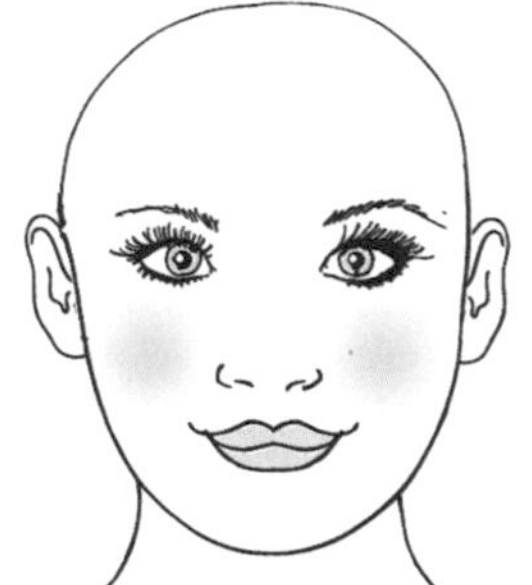

ROUND

Choose styles that will lengthen and frame your face. Long layers are good, but avoid a straight fringe or a short bob.

DO!

Choose a hairstyle that suits your personality and lifestyle. If you struggle to get out of bed in the morning, don't go for a haircut that needs lots of styling and might make you late for school!

HAIR FLAIR

When it comes to creating a specific look, up the style stakes with a carefully chosen hair accessory.

- Glam it up with some sparkly hair slides.
- Nothing beats pretty flowers in the hair for Boho chic.
- For a fun and sporty style, pull your hair off your face with a hairband and pop on a visor.
- Add a cute Alice band for a sweet and delicate look.

BUYING GUIDE

Follow these hair-accessory dos and don'ts to make sure you shop smart.

DO

- Match the accessory to the occasion. Sparkles and flowers are best for parties – while headbands help keep things casual.
- Contrast your hair accessory with your hair colour to ensure it stands out.
- Try on your new hair accessory before your planned event – some can be tricky to get right!

TURN TO PAGE 20 TO MAKE YOUR OWN UNIQUE HAIR ACCESSORIES!

DON'T

- Wear too many accessories at once.
- Buy loads of trendy hair accessories. It's fun to have a few, but make sure you also buy timeless accessories, like a black hairband or a diamante slide, that will last.
- Be afraid to try something new. Have fun experimenting with accessories you've never worn before – ask to borrow your friends' so you can try before you buy.

DIY HAIR ACCESSORIES

WHAT YOU NEED:

- Glue
- Needle and thread
- 2 x 50cm of rickrack
- Scissors

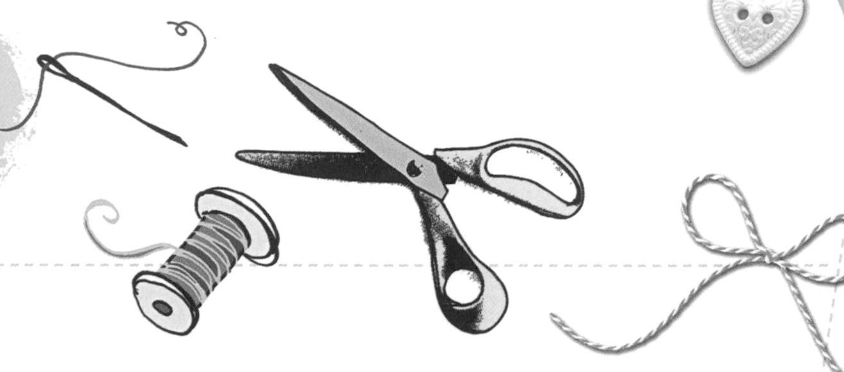

1. Take the two pieces of rickrack and glue or sew together at one end.

2. Lock in each curve of the first piece with the second, then wrap them over and under each other, like a braid, until the two lengths are locked together. Glue or stitch at the end to hold in place.

3. Take an end and start coiling it round itself. Secure it with a little dot of glue every couple of centimetres.

4. When you have coiled it all, tuck the tail end behind and glue to fasten in place.

5. Use your fingers to flip some of the petals outwards.

6. Make as many as you like, then glue or stitch them to your hairbands or slides.

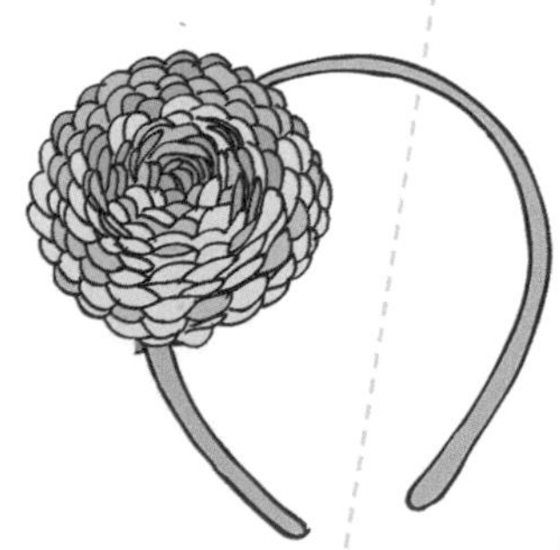

RIBBON BOWS

MAKE THE PERFECT BOW ACCESSORY FOR YOUR HAIR.

WHAT YOU NEED:

- Glue
- Needle and thread
- 50cm of ribbon
- Scissors
- Buttons to decorate

1.

1. Fold your ribbon in half and crease with your thumb, then lay flat. Bring one end of the ribbon to the centre and lay on top of the crease, to form a loop.

2.

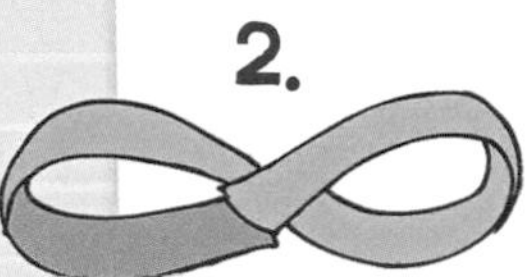

2. Repeat at the other end so your ribbon forms a figure of eight, with two loops. Make sure your ribbon ends overlap.

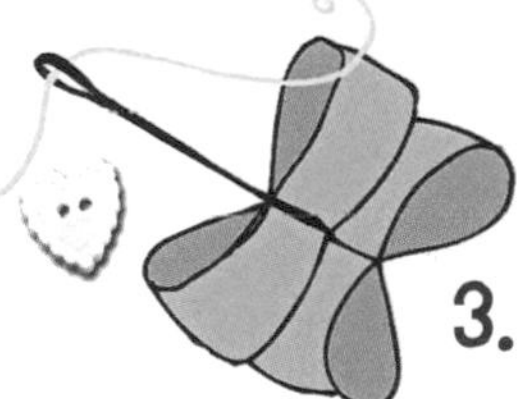

3.

3. Bring the outside edges of each loop into the centre of the figure of eight and pinch the centre of the ribbon loops together.

4.

4. Wrap a piece of thread around the middle and tie in a knot to secure. Sew or stick on a button for a great finishing touch.

CUSTOMIZE YOUR HAIRBANDS AND SLIDES.

3 WAYS TO TRANSFORM AN ALICE BAND

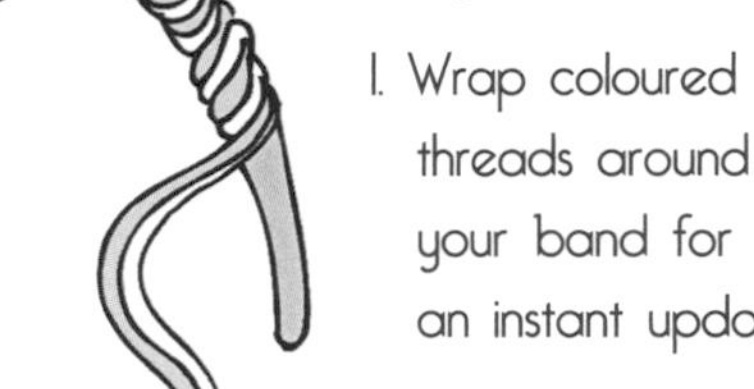

1. Wrap coloured threads around your band for an instant update.

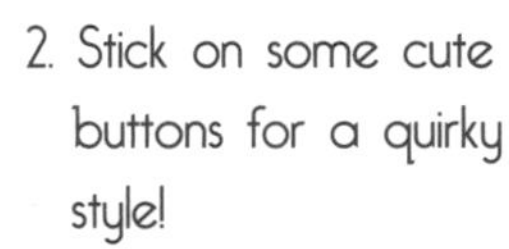

2. Stick on some cute buttons for a quirky style!

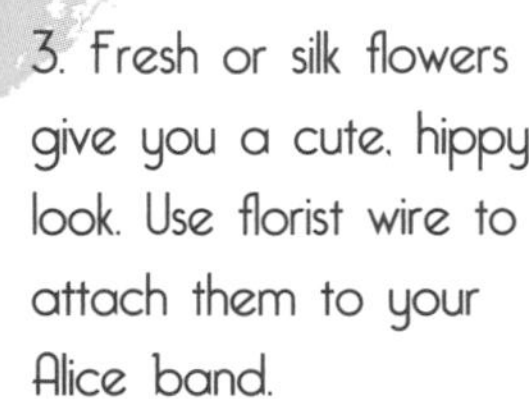

3. Fresh or silk flowers give you a cute, hippy look. Use florist wire to attach them to your Alice band.

A BEGINNER'S GUIDE TO MAKE-UP

When it comes to make-up, working out what to wear and how to wear it can be a bit daunting, so check out these tips and tricks to get you started.

If you are new to make-up, you only need the basics in your make-up bag.

- Eyes = mascara + eyeliner + eye shadow
- Face = tinted moisturizer + blusher + concealer
- Lips = lip balm + lipstick + lip gloss

CREATE YOUR MASTERPIECE

You've got the kit... now you need to apply it!

1. Prep your skin by making sure it's clean and apply a good moisturizer.
2. Rub in your tinted moisturizer. If you have dark circles under the eyes, add a few dots of concealer to lighten.
3. Next come the eyes. Apply eye shadow, eyeliner and then mascara – in that order.
4. Apply some colour to your lips with a lipstick, lip balm or lip gloss.
5. Finish off with a light sweep of blusher. Apply it to the apples of your cheeks, which are the round bits that pop out when you smile.

COLOUR CODE

Finding the perfect eye shadow can be tricky, but the chart below will help you get it right.

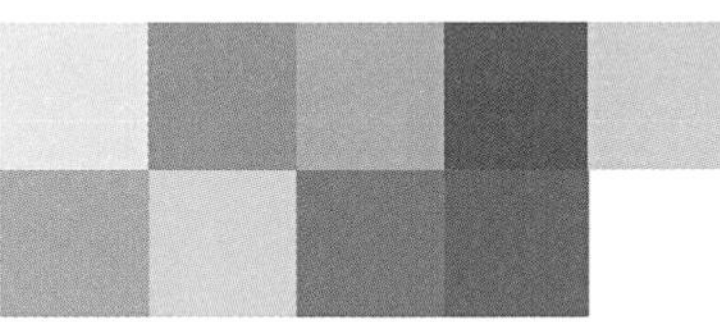

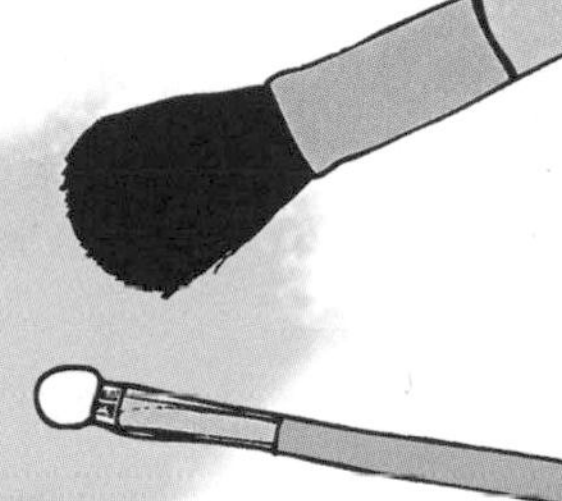

CLEAN UP!

Keeping your brushes clean is easy.

1. Run your brushes under lukewarm water, washing away all the make-up.
2. Fill a bowl with water and add a squirt of shampoo. Gently swirl your brushes in the water.
3. Rinse your brushes under running water again, until the water runs clear.
4. Use a cloth to pat your brushes dry and leave to dry completely overnight before using again.

TURN TO PAGE 30 FOR MORE MAKE-UP TIPS AND TRICKS.

Use dirty brushes to apply your make-up. Clean and replace them regularly for the best results and to stop any skin irritations or infections.

DO IT!

TRANSFORM YOUR EYES

BIGGER AND BETTER

Create the look of bigger, brighter eyes in **FIVE** easy steps.

1. Wearing two shades of eye shadow will really make your eyes pop. Use the darker colour on the outer corner and the lighter shade on the inner one – then gently blend together.

2. Use white eye shadow near your tear ducts (inner corners of your eye) to brighten your eyes.

3. Dark eyeliner will make the whites of your eyes seem brighter and make your eyes look bigger.

4. Curl your eyelashes to open your eyes wider. Begin at the root of the lashes and hold the curler together for about ten seconds. Then move the curler out to the end of your eyelashes and repeat.

5. Apply mascara by placing the wand at the base of your lashes. Sweep the wand up and repeat two or three times to get the thickness you require.

YOU CAN ALWAYS MAKE SOME EYE MAKE-UP STENCILS TO CREATE SOME COOL DESIGNS. USE EYELINERS, LIP LINERS AND GLITTER GEL FOR THE BEST RESULTS.

EYE TREATMENTS

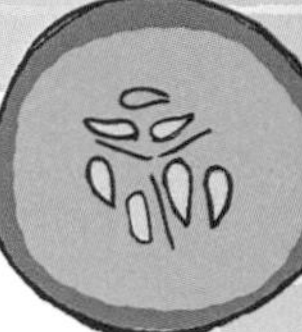

WHAT TO DO

Place two cold cucumber slices over your eyes for five to ten minutes.

Soak two cotton-wool balls in milk and place them over your eyes for five to ten minutes.

Place two teaspoons in the fridge overnight, then place on your eyes for five minutes in the morning.

WHY DO iT

Cold cucumber slices contain antioxidants, that stop damage to skin cells and soothe irritated eyes.

Cold milk has a cool, calming effect on puffy eyes and its fat helps moisturize dry skin.

The cold metal will firm up your skin before you apply make-up.

SHAPE UP

All good make-up artists know that the eyebrows are an important feature on the face. They can lift the eyes and widen or narrow your face, so read on to get the best brows ever.

A - The inner edge of the eyebrow should line up with the outside of your nostril.

B - The highest point of your arch should be in line with the outer edge of your eyeball.

C - The outer edge of your eyebrow should finish here.

D - Get rid of any stray hairs, to create an arch above your eyelid.

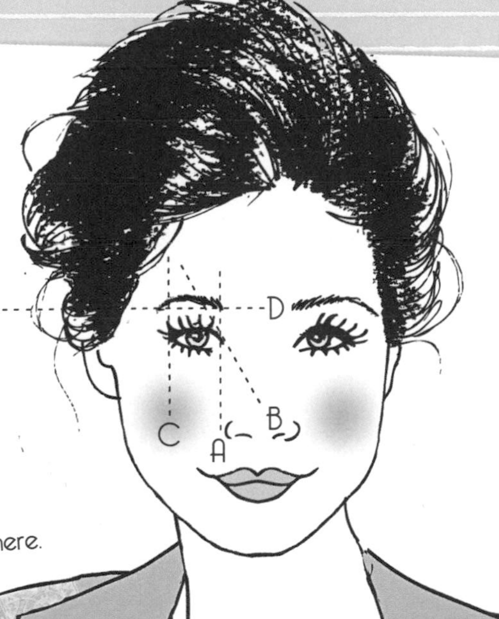

MY BEAUTY ROUTINE

Month ....

BEAUTY FORECAST

What's on (parties / events / trips out)	When	Beauty buys & tries (I will try... I will buy...)
....	....	....
....	....	....
....	....	....
....	....	....
....	....	....

BEAUTY BESTIE

Describe the best beauty product you tried and tested this month.

Top beauty product: ....

It is perfect for my: ....

face ☐ body ☐ hair ☐

nails ☐ other ☐

Rate it: ☐ / 10

DRAW OR STICK A PIC OF IT HERE.

DID YOU KNOW?

The first mascara was created by a French chemist called Eugène Rimmel. It became so popular that 'rimmel' is the word for mascara in several languages.

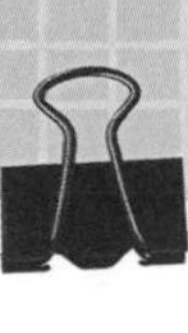

MIRROR, MIRROR, ON THE WALL...

...who's the fairest of them all? Whose beauty style did you like this month? Draw or stick a pic of them here.

Don't forget the little extras to help you create the **WOW** factor!

Best look on a friend was ....

....

My fave celeb look was ....

....

BEAUTY PASS-ON

What's the best beauty tip you heard this month?

....

....

I heard it from my...

friend..

sister..

mum..

gran..

other..

COOL COLOUR

Show your fave eye-shadow colour here. Turn to page 25 to find out which colour eye shadow suits you best.

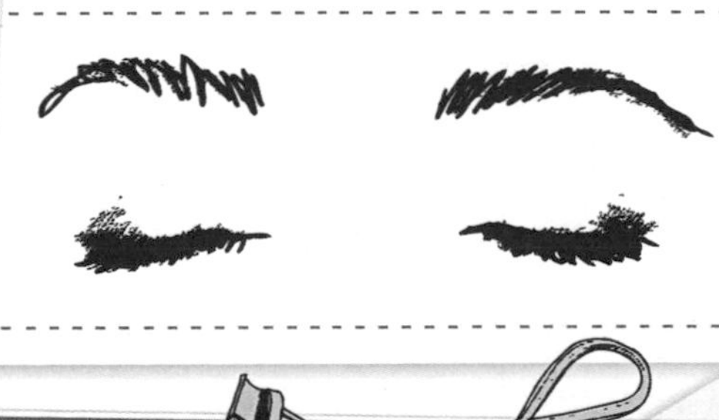

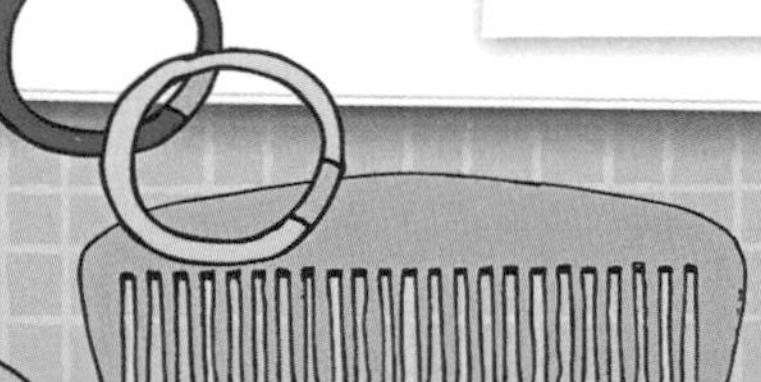

CHEEKS AND LIPS

Check out these tips and tricks on how to get the best results with your make-up.

BRUSH UP!

Brighten up dull skin with a burst of blusher.

- Dark skin tone with warm undertones should go for browns and deep corals.

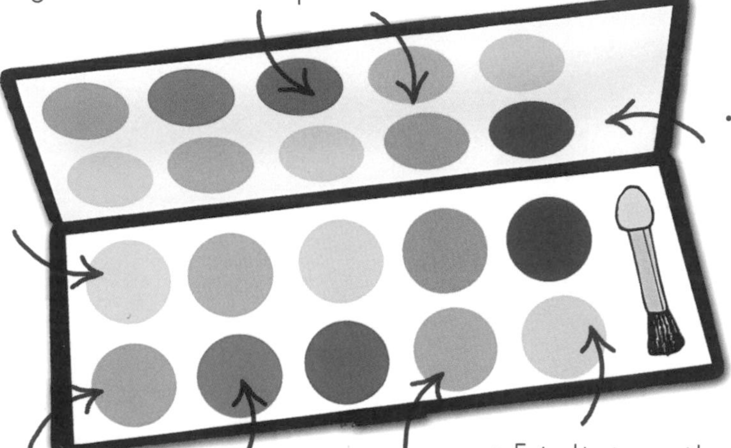

- Fair skin tone with cool undertones? Go for pale pinks with hints of beige, and soft rose.
- Dark skin tone with cool undertones should plump for plum, grape and dark raspberry.
- Medium skin tone with cool undertones should opt for cranberry or light rasberry.
- Medium skin tone with warm undertones should go for soft coral with a hint of brown.
- Fair skin tone with warm undertones? Go for light peach with a touch of pink.

X MARKS THE SPOT

Where blusher should go depends on the shape of your face. Discover your perfect beauty spot here.

LONG FACE

HEART FACE

ROUND FACE

SQUARE FACE

OVAL FACE

LIP BALM

Tinted balms offer a hint of colour and some delicious fruity flavours. Great for dry or chapped lips and perfect for everyday wear.

LIP GLOSS

Choose from sheer, full and shimmer lip gloss for a great, glossy finish. Perfect for dry lips, but you may have to re-apply often as they don't last long!

LIP STAIN

Once applied, a lip stain can last up to ten hours! This is the choice for you if you don't like the feel or taste of lipstick.

LIPSTICK

Opt for a chic matte finish or a glamorous gloss. Great if you like variety as there are lots of colours to choose from - save for a special occasion.

DO!

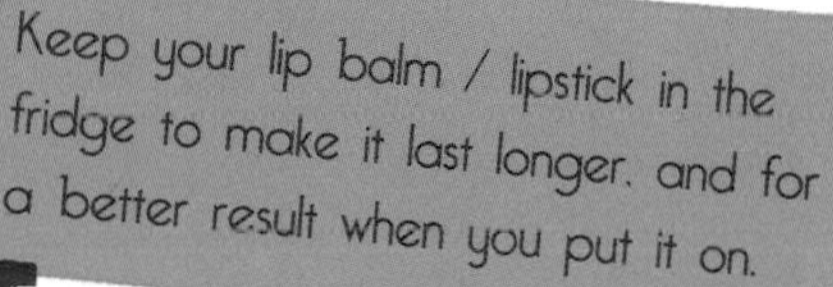

PERSONALITY POUT

Take this quick quiz to find your perfect lipstick...

1. When you pack for your holiday you like to...
a) plan your outfits for each day and pack what you need.
b) pack only the essentials.
c) take twice as many outfits as you'll ever get to wear.

2. Your perfect party outfit would be...
a) something pink and girly.
b) a casual and comfy dress or skirt.
c) an ultra-glam dress that screams: 'Look at me!'.

3. When you get up in the morning you...
a) take about ten minutes to get ready.
b) usually leave the house without looking in a mirror.
c) plan your beauty routine like a military operation - which takes about an hour!

Mostly **As** - a super-sweet pink lip gloss will create the perfect look for you.
Mostly **Bs** - you need a quick and practical lip solution, so try a fruit lip balm.
Mostly **Cs** - stand out from the crowd with a bright red or pink lipstick.

TURN THE PAGE TO SEE HOW TO CREATE THE PERFECT POUT!

DO IT!

PERFECT POUT!

Make the most of your lips with these simple tips and tricks.

HOW TO APPLY LIPSTICK

1. Apply a dab of lip balm to your lips, as dry and cracked lips won't hold colour for long.

2. Outline your lips with a lip liner to stop your lipstick colour running. Pick one that is either the same shade or lighter than your lipstick colour.

3. Apply a coat of your lipstick.

4. Finish with a shiny lip gloss or pat dry with a tissue for a chic, matte look.

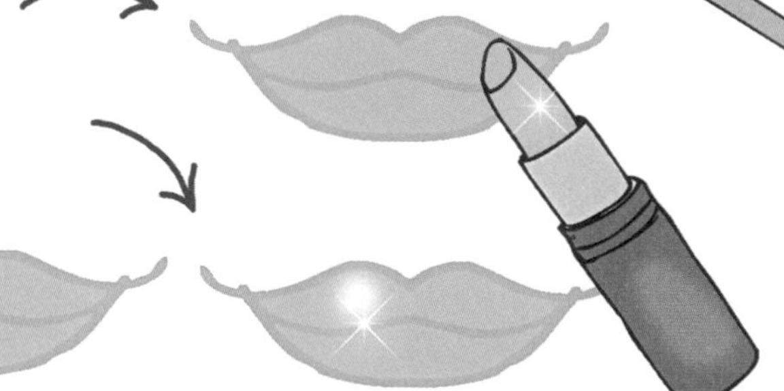

THREE TIPS FOR HEALTHY LIPS

1. Exfoliate your lips by gently rubbing them with a dry toothbrush.

2. Polish your lips with some lip balm. For best results, wear overnight.

3. Drink plenty of water to prevent cracked and dry dehydrated lips.

1.

2.

3.

DO

- Let your lips do the talking... opt for a bold and bright lip colour and wear minimal make-up on your eyes and cheeks.
- Opt for a lip colour darker than your skin, to avoid looking washed out.
- Match your make-up. If you are going for a neutral shade, keep the rest of your face natural too.

DON'T

- Forget to brush your teeth before applying lipstick. Yellow teeth and bright lips are not a good look!
- Colour your lips outside their natural shape, unless, of course, you're thinking of becoming a clown!

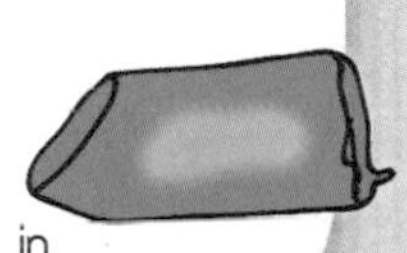

- Pick a shade just because it's fashionable. Find one that suits you, and you feel comfortable in.

THE CURSE OF THE COLD SORE

Cold sores can be painful and embarrassing, and they always show up at the worst times! Put a stop to painful cold sores with these simple tips.

- Keep healthy – cold sores strike when you are tired and your immune system is low. Eating well, exercising, sleeping and drinking plenty of water will help fight off an attack.
- Protect your face and lips from the sun with lip balm and sun lotion.
- The amino acid arginine helps promote cold sore outbreaks – so avoid foods that are rich in this when you're feeling run down, like nuts, spinach and (sadly) chocolate!

MY BEAUTY ROUTINE

Month ....

BEAUTY FORECAST

What's on (parties / events / trips out)	When	Beauty buys & tries (I will try... I will buy...)
....	....	....
....	....	....
....	....	....
....	....	....
....	....	....

BEAUTY BESTIE

Describe the best beauty product you tried and tested this month.

Top beauty product: ....

It is perfect for my: ....

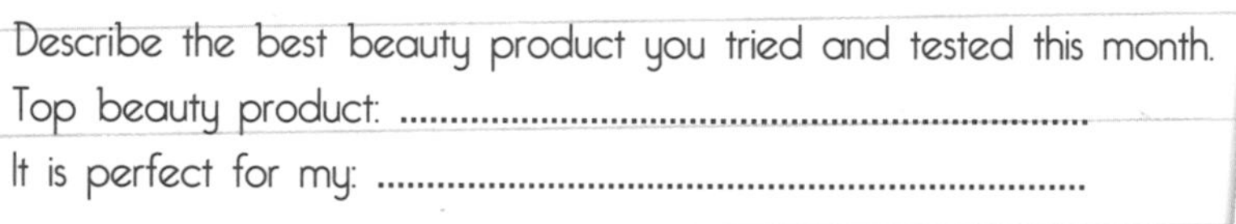

face ☐ body ☐ hair ☐

nails ☐ other ☐

Rate it: ☐ / 10

DRAW OR STICK A PIC OF IT HERE.

DID YOU KNOW?

The first lipsticks were made thousands of years ago, when women used to grind precious gems and decorate their lips with their dust!

Don't forget the little extras to help you create the **WOW** factor!

Best look on a friend was ....
....

MIRROR, MIRROR, ON THE WALL...

...who's the fairest of them all? Whose beauty style did you like this month? Draw or stick a pic of them here.

My fave celeb look was ....
....

You've nailed your hair and make-up... now design the perfect outfit.

LIP-TASTIC

Rate these lipstick colours with 1 for the best and 10 for the worst, to show your preference.

BODY BEAUTIFUL

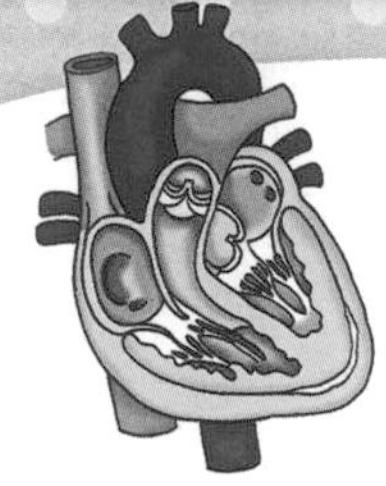

READ ON TO LOOK GREAT ON THE OUTSIDE AND FEEL GOOD ON THE INSIDE TOO!

WORK IT OUT!

Exercise is a great way to keep healthy and strong. Aerobic exercise like running, swimming or dancing will get your heart pumping, which helps it get better at its main job – delivering oxygen around your body. Exercise is also scientifically proven to put you in a good mood. When you exercise, your brain releases chemicals called endorphins that make you feel happy. So what are you waiting for? On your marks, get set, go!

HOW TO GET PERFECT POSTURE...

Good posture can make you look and feel more confident (and prevent knee, back and hip pain when you are older). Get it right in **THREE** easy steps.

1. Sit up straight by uncrossing your legs and planting your feet on the floor. Your neck and head should be in line with your spine.

2. When you stand, make sure you balance your weight between each foot, relax your shoulders and pull your belly button towards your spine.

3. Don't text while you walk – it can affect your movement and stability. It also forces you to hunch over, which is bad for your spine (plus you might bump into a lamp-post!).

DO!

Make sure you drink plenty of water after exercise to help you rehydrate.

SKIN SECRETS

Keeping your skin soft and supple is easy when you know how...

1. Warm water is best for cleaning your skin. Just make sure it's not too hot as this can irritate your skin.

2. Gently pat, rather than rub, your face dry with a clean towel so you don't pull on your skin.

3. Exfoliate before you moisturize, as this will remove dead skin cells, clearing the way for your moisturizer to do its job.

4. Always moisturize your skin after a bath or shower – this helps lock in the moisture and stops your skin from drying out.

5. Your elbows and knees may need an extra rub with moisturizing cream, as they can dry out easily.

6. Always protect your skin in the sun. Slip on a hat, slop on a T-shirt and slap on some sun lotion to keep it healthy.

BODY ART

Turn your body into a work of art with temporary tattoos. Impress your friends with your cool designs.

TURN THE PAGE FOR SOME FANTASTIC YOGA POSITIONS TO KEEP YOUR BODY TONED AND CHILL YOUR MIND.

BODY BALANCE

Take time out each day to relax your mind and strengthen your body with these easy yoga moves.

1. **MOUNTAIN POSE**

How to do it:

Stand with your feet hip width apart and your arms by your side. Breathe deeply and evenly as you raise your arms up and stretch them towards the sky.

WHAT DOES IT DO? Improves your posture.

HOW HARD IS IT? Easy-peasy.

2. **DOWNWARD DOG**

How to do it:

Get on your hands and knees and walk your hands forward. Straighten your legs, so your body makes an upside-down V shape.

WHAT DOES IT DO? Great for stretching your calves.

HOW HARD IS IT? Quite easy.

3. **WARRIOR POSE**

How to do it:

Stand with your legs apart. Turn out your right foot 90 degrees and your left foot in slightly. Stretch your arms out with your palms down. Lunge into your right knee.

WHAT DOES IT DO? Strengthens and stretches your legs and ankles.

HOW HARD IS IT? Takes a bit of practice.

4. **TREE POSE**

How to do it:

Start in the mountain pose, then shift your weight on to your left leg. Place the sole of your right foot inside your left thigh and find your balance. Bring your hands into a prayer position. Repeat on the other leg.

WHAT DOES IT DO? Improves your balance.

HOW HARD IS IT? Practice makes perfect.

5. **COBRA POSE**

How to do it:

Lie on the floor with your hands underneath your shoulders, legs extended and the tops of your feet on the floor. Push up and lift your chest off the ground.

WHAT DOES IT DO? Strengthens spine, arms and wrists.

HOW HARD IS IT? Takes a bit of practice.

6. **BOAT POSE**

How to do it:

Sit on the floor with your legs straight in front of you. Lean back, lifting your legs. Stretch your arms to the front, with your palms facing your body.

WHAT DOES IT DO? Strengthens spine and tummy.

HOW HARD IS IT? Practice makes perfect.

7. **SEATED FORWARD BEND**

How to do it:

Sit on the floor and slowly bend your body towards your knees, with your head down and arms outstretched. Only go as far as feels comfortable.

WHAT DOES IT DO? Helps relieve stress.

HOW HARD IS IT? Takes a bit of practice.

8. **EASY POSE**

How to do it:

Sit up straight, on the floor, with your legs crossed in front of you. Rest your hands on your knees.

WHAT DOES IT DO? Aligns and strengthens your spine.

HOW HARD IS IT? Easy-peasy!

MY BEAUTY ROUTINE

Month ....

BEAUTY FORECAST

What's on (parties / events / trips out)	When	Beauty buys & tries (I will try... I will buy...)
....	....	....
....	....	....
....	....	....
....	....	....
....	....	....

BEAUTY BESTIE

Describe the best beauty product you tried and tested this month.

Top beauty product: ....

It is perfect for my: ....

face ☐ body ☐ hair ☐

nails ☐ other ☐

Rate it: ☐ / 10

DRAW OR STICK A PIC OF IT HERE.

DID YOU KNOW?

Wearing the wrong shoes can damage your spine.
Pick comfy shoes that will support your spine and body.
Save heels for special occasions!

Don't forget the little extras to help you create the **WOW** factor!

My fave celeb look was ....
....
....

BEAUTY PASS-ON

What's the best beauty tip you heard this month?

....

....

I heard it from my...
friend..............................
sister..............................
mum..............................
gran..............................
other..............................

Best look on a friend was ....
....

MIRROR, MIRROR, ON THE WALL...

...who's the fairest of them all? Whose beauty style did you like this month? Draw or stick a pic of them here.

DESIGNER DOODLES

Draw some body-art designs below

NAIL IT!

If you're guilty of a bit of nail-nibbling, read on for tips and tricks on how to get perfect nails.

HOW TO KEEP YOUR NAILS STRONG

Check out these top tips on how to grow strong, healthy nails.

- Eat a well-balanced diet. Nails are made of protein, so add to their strength by eating lots of chicken, fish and spinach.
- Regular manicures (turn to page 44 to find out how!).
- Moisturize your hands every time you wash them.
- Wear gloves when it's cold to stop your nails and hands becoming dry and damaged.

DON'T

- Cut your cuticles as they protect your nails from infection – push them back instead.
- Use nails as tools to open letters... use a pair of scissors.
- Peel off old polish. It will damage your nails. Always use a nail-polish remover.
- Never file back and forth. File your nails from the outside edge to the centre so you don't weaken them.

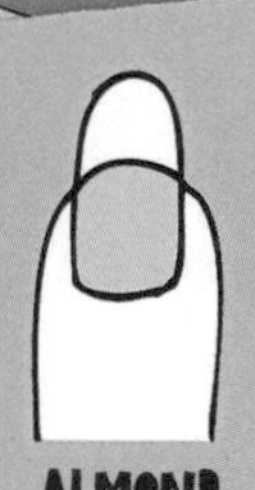

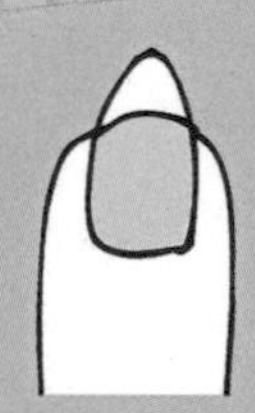

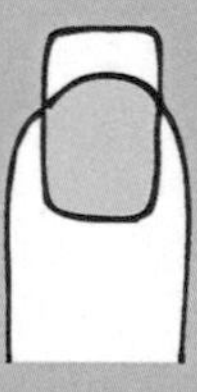

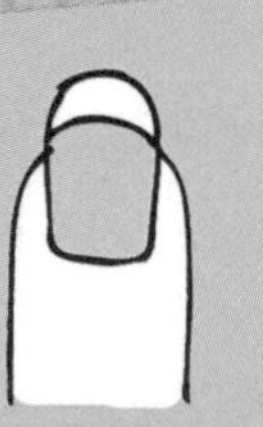

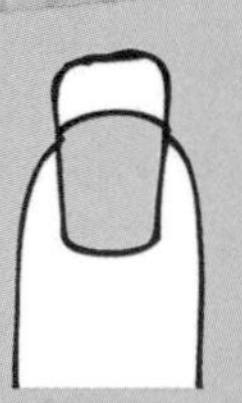

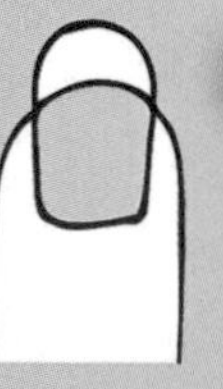

HOW TO SHAPE YOUR NAILS

- Pick a shape you like.
- Take a nail file and file your nails from the outside edge to the centre.
- Only file in one direction, and only file when your nails are dry.

PERFECT POLISH

Painting your nails has never been so much fun – experiment with polish, glitter and nail stickers to create the coolest designs. Try these clever tips and tricks on your nails!

1. Use a bit of netting to create this nifty effect.

- Paint your nails with a base coat and let it half dry.
- Place a small piece of netting (or you can use a piece of fishnet tights) over the nail and sponge on a second colour or glitter. Leave to dry, then peel off netting.

DO!

Layer up nail-polish colours to make your nails look longer.

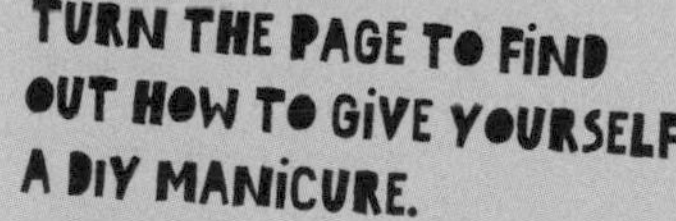

TURN THE PAGE TO FIND OUT HOW TO GIVE YOURSELF A DIY MANICURE.

2. Glam up your nail design by dipping half-dry nails in a pot of glitter.

3. Use a toothpick to create a pretty heart shape on your nails.

- Dip your toothpick into your pot of nail polish and create a dot.
- Place a second dot next to it.
- Add a third dot underneath.
- Use your toothpick to blend the dots together to form your heart.

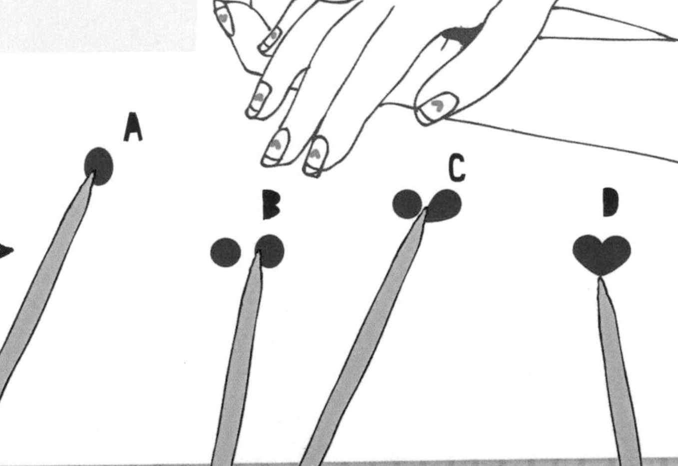

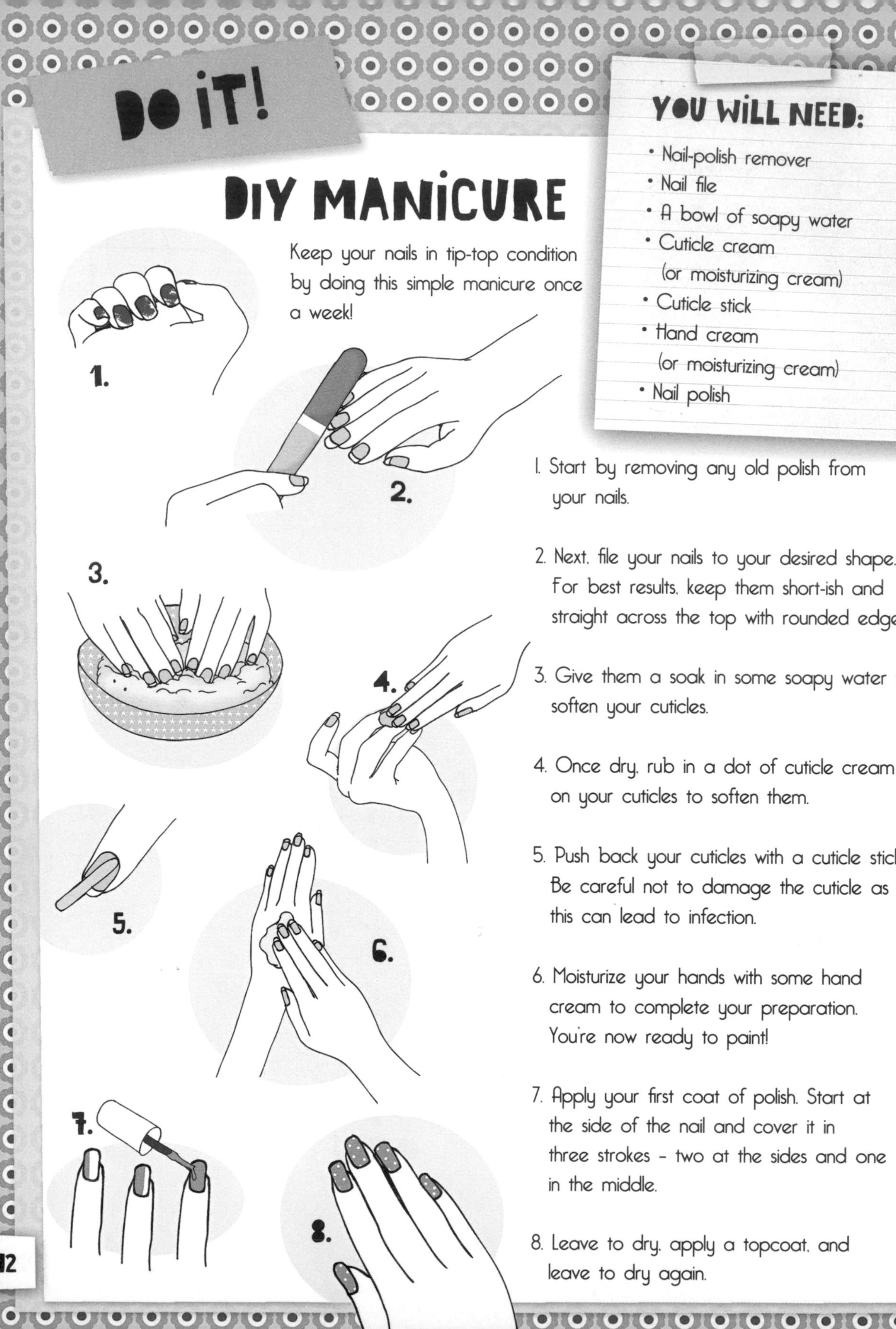

DIY MANICURE

Keep your nails in tip-top condition by doing this simple manicure once a week!

YOU WILL NEED:

- Nail-polish remover
- Nail file
- A bowl of soapy water
- Cuticle cream (or moisturizing cream)
- Cuticle stick
- Hand cream (or moisturizing cream)
- Nail polish

1. Start by removing any old polish from your nails.

2. Next, file your nails to your desired shape. For best results, keep them short-ish and straight across the top with rounded edges.

3. Give them a soak in some soapy water to soften your cuticles.

4. Once dry, rub in a dot of cuticle cream on your cuticles to soften them.

5. Push back your cuticles with a cuticle stick. Be careful not to damage the cuticle as this can lead to infection.

6. Moisturize your hands with some hand cream to complete your preparation. You're now ready to paint!

7. Apply your first coat of polish. Start at the side of the nail and cover it in three strokes - two at the sides and one in the middle.

8. Leave to dry, apply a topcoat, and leave to dry again.

PRACTICE MAKES PERFECT!

Once you've nailed a simple manicure, why not try out these cool nail designs? Don't forget to have your nail-polish remover handy, as some are a bit tricky and will take a couple of goes to get right.

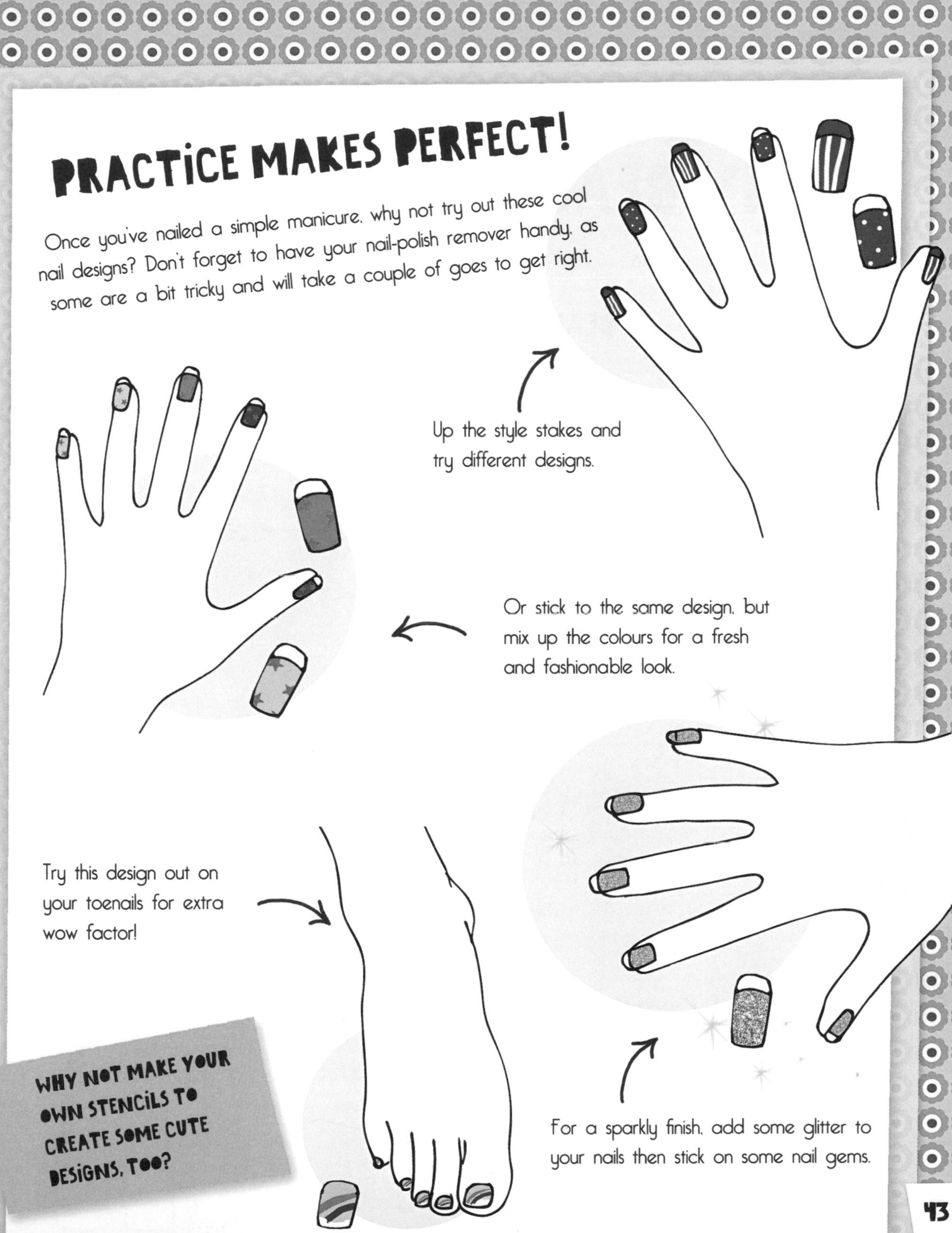

Up the style stakes and try different designs.

Or stick to the same design, but mix up the colours for a fresh and fashionable look.

Try this design out on your toenails for extra wow factor!

For a sparkly finish, add some glitter to your nails then stick on some nail gems.

WHY NOT MAKE YOUR OWN STENCILS TO CREATE SOME CUTE DESIGNS, TOO?

MY BEAUTY ROUTINE

Month ....

BEAUTY FORECAST

What's on (parties / events / trips out)	When	Beauty buys & tries (I will try... I will buy...)
....	....	....
....	....	....
....	....	....
....	....	....
....	....	....

BEAUTY BESTIE

Describe the best beauty product you tried and tested this month.
Top beauty product: ....
It is perfect for my: ....

face ☐ body ☐ hair ☐

nails ☐ other ☐

Rate it: ☐ / 10

DRAW OR STICK A PIC OF IT HERE.

DID YOU KNOW?

Your nails are made of the same stuff as your hair - keratin - which means the foods that are good for your hair; will give you strong and healthy nails, too.

Don't forget the little extras to help you create the **WOW** factor!

Doodle some pretty earrings to make the most of an up-do!

BEAUTY PASS-ON

What's the best beauty tip you heard this month?

....

....

I heard it from my...

friend..

sister..

mum..

gran..

other..

PERFECT POLISH

Rate these nail colours with 1 for the best and 10 for the worst, to show your preference.

YOU ARE WHAT YOU EAT

No matter how hard you try, if you don't feel good on the inside you won't look good on the outside. Read on to discover healthy-eating secrets that will help you look (and feel) great.

EAT YOURSELF BEAUTIFUL

The key to being healthy and looking good is to eat a balanced diet. Use the chart below to make sure you're eating the right amount of each food group.

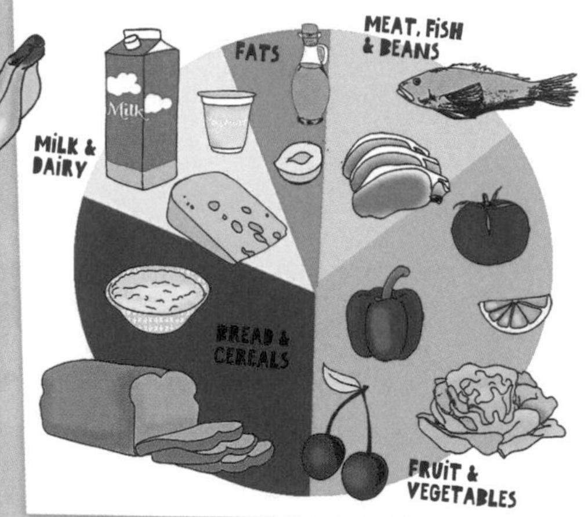

REVIVE WITH FIVE!

Eating at least five portions of fruit and veg a day is a great way to keep healthy and stay beautiful. Try these nifty ways to get your five a day!

1. Add some chopped bananas or berries to your morning cereal.
2. Make your own smoothies, packed with yummy fruit and calcium.
3. You don't have to eat just fresh veg. A portion of tinned baked beans will do the job, too.
4. Use fruit or veg when you bake – add courgettes or carrots to your cakes, or berries and raisins to your cookies. Yum!
5. Swap a sandwich for a delicious veggie soup.

BEAUTY BOOSTERS

Some foods are better for you than others. Read on for what to munch on to help you look your best.

1. Inside just one almond you'll find skin-boosting zinc and hair- and bone-strengthening calcium.
2. Spinach will boost the collagen in your skin, making it look and feel better.
3. Tuck into pumpkin seeds to strengthen your nails.
4. Bananas are high in potassium, which will help get rid of tired eyes.
5. The antioxidants in green tea will help give you a great complexion.

SAY CHEESE!

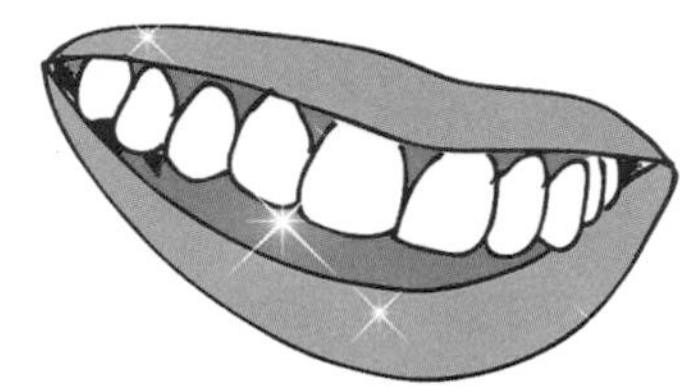

Lipstick may help create the perfect pout, but for a truly great grin, you need to take care of your teeth and gums too.

- Brush and floss twice a day. Using a fluoride toothpaste will also help harden your teeth and prevent decay.
- Milk, greens and almonds are packed with calcium, which will keep your teeth and gums healthy.
- Opt for water over sugary and acidic drinks, like fizzy drinks and fruit juices.
- Casein protein, found in cheese, will strengthen your teeth.
- Chew on raw veggies, as this helps produce lots of saliva to fight germs in your mouth and prevent bad breath.

DO!

Try a tasty coconut. Its high levels of Omega 3 and essential fatty acids will help your hair grow and keep your skin soft and supple.

WATER WORKS

Water makes up around half of your body weight and helps you fight off illness and carry blood around your body. Staying hydrated keeps your brain alert and active and your skin looking great. So make sure you drink a glass or two of water with every meal and snack, plus extra when it's hot outside.

TURN THE PAGE FOR SOME SCRUMMY RECIPES.

EAT WELL

SALMON PASTA
(serves 4)

WHAT YOU NEED:

- 200g pasta
- 200g salmon
- 6 tablespoons of crème fraiche
- 1 tin of chopped tomatoes
- A handful of grated cheese (Parmesan is best)
- A knob of butter

Grab your apron and chopping board for quick and easy recipes that taste great and are good for you too!

WHAT TO DO:

1. Cook the pasta in a large pan of water, according to the instructions on the packet (ask an adult to help).
2. Wrap the salmon in some foil with a knob of butter and cook in the oven at 180 degrees / Gas Mark 5 for 15 to 20 minutes.
3. Heat the crème fraiche and the chopped tomatoes in a pan, stirring until blended. Add the cheese, stir until melted, then remove from heat.
4. Remove the salmon from the oven, and break it up into small, bite-size pieces and add it to your sauce. Be careful when you do this, as the salmon will be hot!
5. Drain the pasta and toss together with your sauce. Delicious!

WHY IT'S GOOD FOR YOU:

Salmon is an excellent source of protein, vitamins and minerals. However, its main benefit is that it's good for your heart as oily fish helps blood flow freely around your body. Crème fraiche is a healthy alternative to full-fat cream and tastes just as good.

LITTLE EXTRAS!

Add some chopped spinach to your sauce for an extra boost of iron, it will help keep your hair healthy and strong.

DON'T FORGET TO ASK AN ADULT TO HELP YOU COOK THE PASTA AND USE THE OVEN.

AVOCADO DIP

WHAT YOU NEED:

- 1 ripe avocado
- 1/3 of a cucumber, peeled and grated
- 2 tablespoons of low-fat yoghurt
- Juice of 1/3 lemon
- Cayenne pepper

WHAT TO DO:

1. Mash the avocado and mix in the grated cucumber.
2. Add the rest of the ingredients and mix well.
3. Transfer to a bowl and serve with chopped peppers, carrots, celery or steamed asparagus.

WHY IT'S GOOD FOR YOU:

Avocadoes are a great source of lutein, which works as an antioxidant and prevents eye disease. They also contain vitamins and folic acid that will help keep your heart healthy.

BLUEBERRY SMOOTHIE

WHAT YOU NEED:

- 75g blueberries
- 1 banana
- 100ml of apple juice

WHAT YOU DO:

Add the ingredients to a blender and mix together to make a delicious smoothie. If you don't have a blender, mash up the fruit with a fork then add the apple juice and whisk.

WHY IT'S GOOD FOR YOU:

Blueberries are a superfood and are packed with antioxidants, which help stop damage to your body's cells. They're also said to improve your memory, so snack on them while you study for a test!

MY BEAUTY ROUTINE

Month ....

BEAUTY FORECAST

What's on (parties / events / trips out)	When	Beauty buys & tries (I will try... I will buy...)
....	....	....
....	....	....
....	....	....
....	....	....
....	....	....

BEAUTY BESTIE

Describe the best beauty product you tried and tested this month.

Top beauty product: ....

It is perfect for my: ....

face ☐ body ☐ hair ☐

nails ☐ other ☐

Rate it: ☐ / 10

DRAW OR STICK A PIC OF IT HERE.

DID YOU KNOW?

If you're looking for a super-fruit to munch on, go for a blackberry. It's the fruit with the highest levels of antioxidants and is bursting with vitamins and potassium.

MIRROR, MIRROR, ON THE WALL...

...who's the fairest of them all? Whose beauty style did you like this month? Draw or stick a pic of them here.

BEAUTY PASS-ON

What's the best beauty tip you heard this month?

....

....

I heard it from my...

friend..

sister..

mum..

gran..

other..

Best look on a friend was ....

....

My fave celeb look was ....

....

Don't forget the little extras to help you create the **WOW** factor!

Dish of the day

SUPERFOOD!

The healthiest dish I ate this month was:

....

Draw a pic of it here.

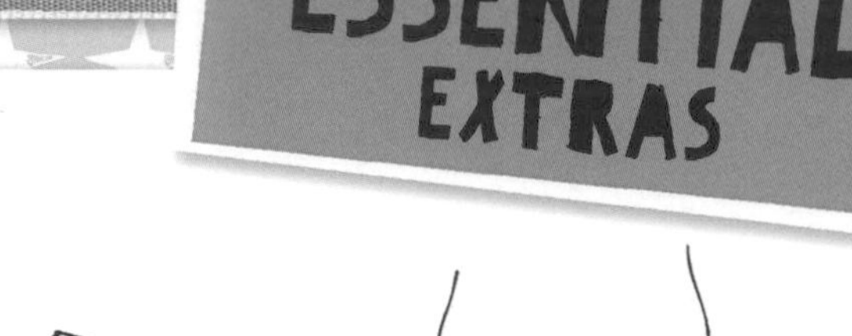

ESSENTIAL EXTRAS

1. Bright skinny belts look great over a cardigan.

2. Wrap a scarf around your waist to update an old dress.

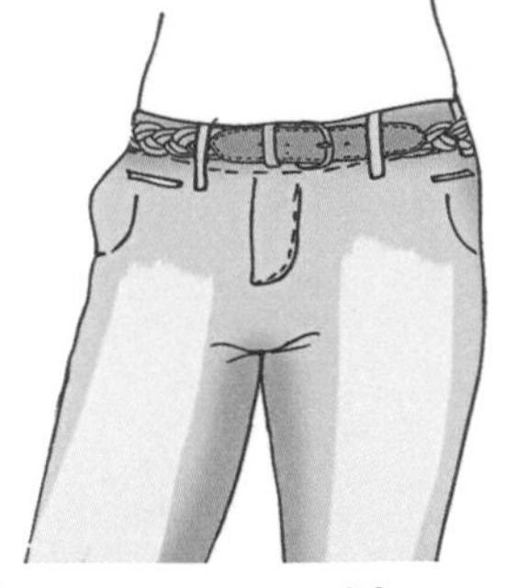

3. Plait some string, ribbons or rope together to create a cool nautical-style belt to wear with your jeans.

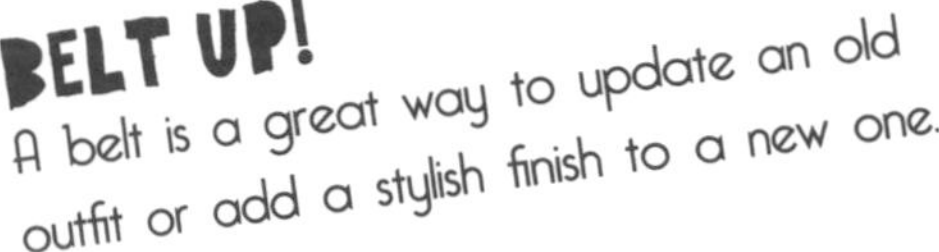

BELT UP!

A belt is a great way to update an old outfit or add a stylish finish to a new one.

HEADS UP!

Top off your look with a stylish hat – just make sure you pick the right one for your face shape!

SQUARE: Choose hats with a floppy or curved brim to help soften your face.

ROUND: Try a fedora! The height and brim are great for your face shape.

OVAL: You look great in all kinds of hats, but avoid tall and narrow ones.

BRING ON THE BLING!

Jewellery is a great way to give your look the wow factor. Try these easy tips and tricks for how to use bling to draw attention to your hair, eyes and clothes.

- If you want to appear taller, opt for a long necklace. Try a choker necklace to make you seem shorter.

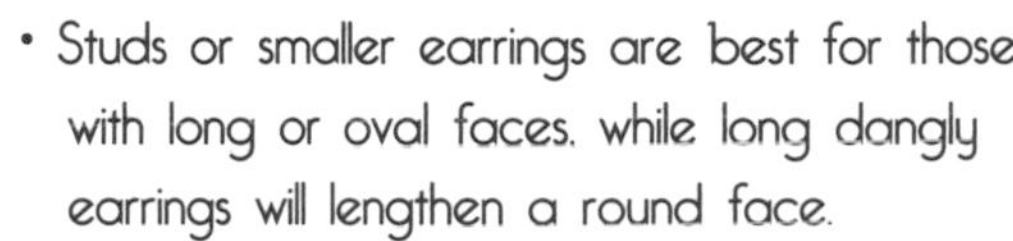

- Studs or smaller earrings are best for those with long or oval faces, while long dangly earrings will lengthen a round face.

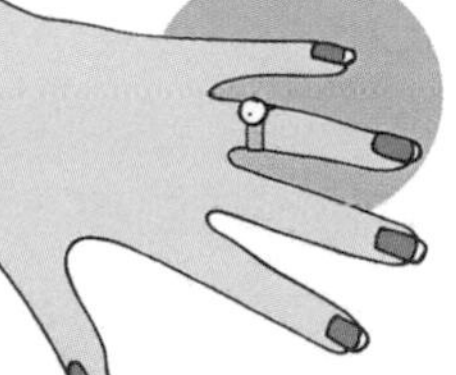
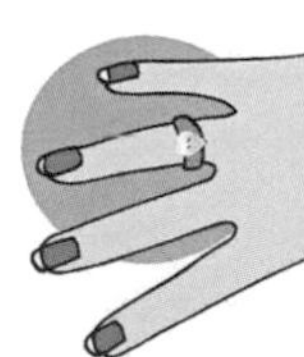

- Gold jewellery looks best on warm-toned skin, while silver will enhance cooler tones.

TURN TO PAGE 7 TO FIND OUT WHETHER YOUR SKIN TONE IS WARM OR COOL.

DON'T

Overload your look with too much clutter. Pick just one part of your face or body you want to highlight. Too many accessories could look messy.

PIERCED EARS

If you've just had your ears pierced (or are hoping to have them done!) read on for three top tips on how to look after them.

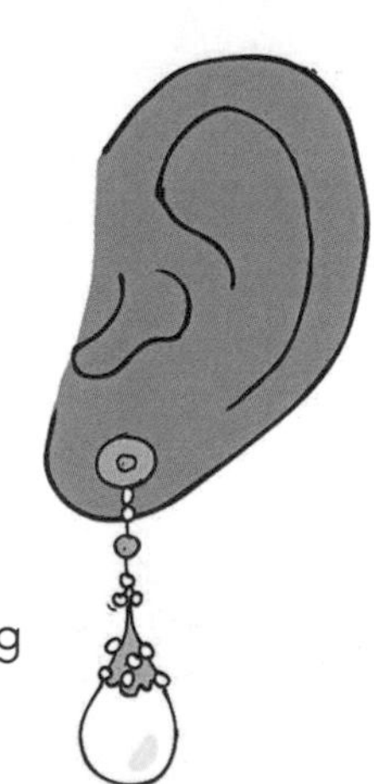

1. Make sure your first earrings have a gold post (the part that slips through your ear) as this will be less likely to cause infection.
2. You will need to leave your first earrings in for up to six weeks, until the holes have healed. That way they won't close up when you remove your earrings.
3. Keep your newly pierced ears infection-free by keeping them clean and rubbing antibiotic ointment on them.

MY BEAUTY ROUTINE

Month ....

BEAUTY FORECAST

What's on (parties / events / trips out)	When	Beauty buys & tries (I will try... I will buy...)
....	....	....
....	....	....
....	....	....
....	....	....
....	....	....

BEAUTY BESTIE

Describe the best beauty product you tried and tested this month.

Top beauty product: ....

It is perfect for my: ....

face ☐ body ☐ hair ☐

nails ☐ other ☐

Rate it: ☐ / 10

DRAW OR STICK A PIC OF IT HERE.

DID YOU KNOW?

Diamonds are formed over billions of years under intense pressure and heat deep underground. They are sometimes brought to the Earth's surface by volcanic eruptions!

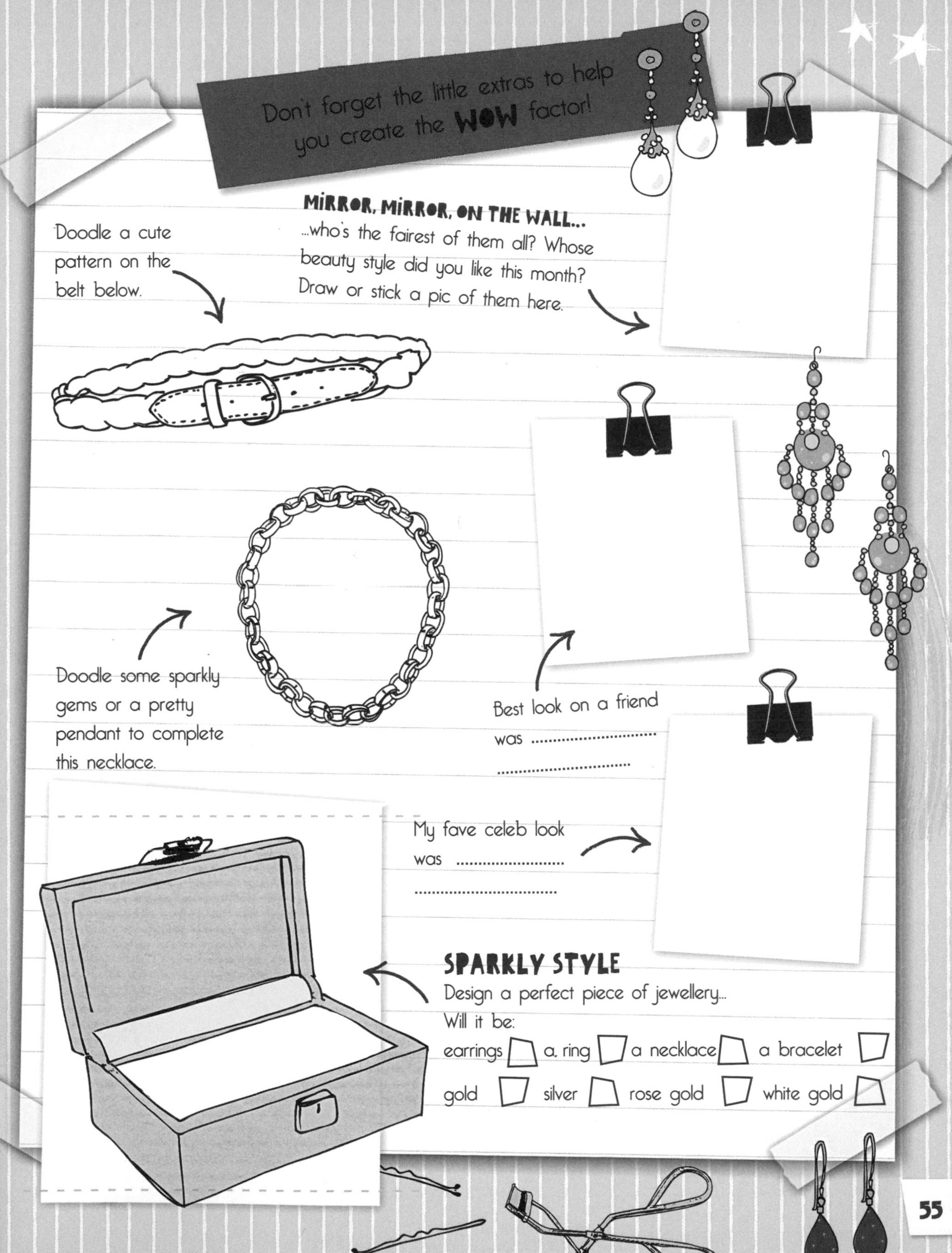
Don't forget the little extras to help you create the WOW factor!
MIRROR, MIRROR, ON THE WALL...
...who's the fairest of them all? Whose beauty style did you like this month? Draw or stick a pic of them here.
Doodle a cute pattern on the belt below.
Doodle some sparkly gems or a pretty pendant to complete this necklace.
Best look on a friend was ....
....
My fave celeb look was ....
....
SPARKLY STYLE
Design a perfect piece of jewellery...
Will it be:
earrings a ring a necklace a bracelet
gold silver rose gold white gold

SCENTS-ATIONAL!

Picking the perfect scent can be tricky, but a little know-how goes a long way!

TYPES OF FRAGRANCE

EAU DE TOILETTE - this type of fragrance contains between 5–15% of essential oils or extracts, so it's quite weak and the scent won't last that long because it's diluted with water.

EAU DE PARFUM - is slightly stronger, using between 10–20% of aromatic oils. It's more potent and lasts longer than eau de toilette.

PARFUM - this is the longest-lasting fragrance, using more than 20% of aromatic essence. It packs a potent punch so should be dabbed, rather than sprayed on.

FRAGRANCE FAMILY

A fragrance family chart is used to describe different scents. There are four main categories - woody, fresh, floral and oriental. A mixture of all four of these categories is called a fougère.

STRAIGHT TO THE POINT

Follow these simple steps on how to apply your perfume.

1. Spray or dab your perfume on to your pulse points. These are the locations in your body where your blood vessels are closest to your skin. These spots radiate heat that will help the fragrance spread from your skin into the air. Your pulse points are on the inner wrists, at the base of your throat, inner elbows and behind your knees and ears.
2. Do not rub your wrists together after applying, as this can crush the scent!
3. Apply your perfume before putting on your clothes as it can stain some fabrics.

Apply some petroleum jelly to your skin before applying your perfume, as it will make your perfume last longer!

WHAT'S YOUR FRAGRANCE PERSONALITY?

Take this quick quiz to find out...

1. After school you love to...
a) get stuck into your homework
b) relax in the garden and get some fresh air
c) eat a healthy snack of fruit and veg
d) just chill out

2. Your friends describe you as...
a) reliable and realistic
b) a bit of a dreamer
c) outgoing and active
d) laid-back and easy-going

TURN THE PAGE TO MAKE YOUR OWN PERFUME TO MATCH YOUR SCENT STYLE.

3. Which fashion style do you like best?
a) smart and clean
b) flirty and floaty
c) sporty and fresh
d) cool and casual

4. Which kind of smell do you love the most?
a) fresh air
b) flowers and fresh-cut grass
c) citrus fruits like lemon and orange
d) home-baked cookies

Mostly **As** - an oriental perfume will add a bit of spice and keep you fresh.
Mosty **Bs** - a floral scent will reflect your emotional and dreamy personality best.
Mostly **Cs** - a fruity fragrance will complement your fun-loving and active lifestyle
Mostly **Ds** - a light, natural and woody scent matches your laid-back attitude.

D IT!

MAKE Y UR OWN PERFUME

WHAT YOU NEED:

- 2 teaspoons of almond oil
- Essential oils of your choice – orange, lavender and peppermint are good ones to start with
- A small lump of beeswax
- An old lip-balm pot

SOLID PERFUME

WHAT TO DO:

1.

Combine about 2 teaspoons of almond oil with your essential oils. Add a drop or two of your essential oils at a time, until you have the scent you like.

2.

Melt a small chunk of beeswax in a glass dish in the microwave.

3.

Once melted, add the oil mixture and stir to combine.

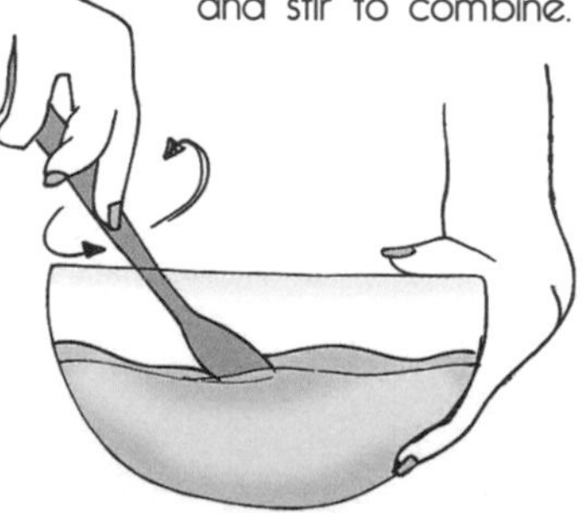

4.

Pour into a small container (like an old lip-balm pot) and leave to harden.

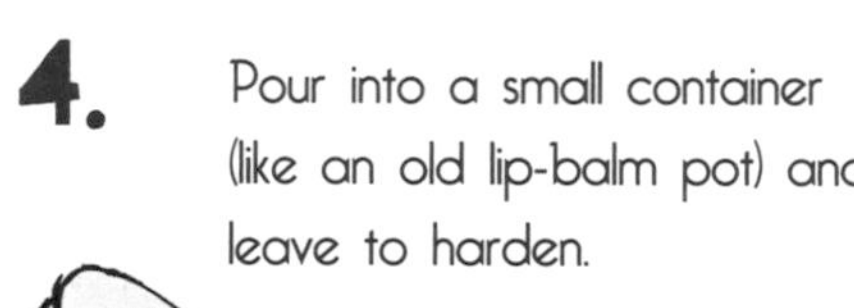

DON'T FORGET TO ASK AN ADULT TO HELP YOU MELT THE BEESWAX.

LIQUID PERFUME

WHAT YOU NEED:

- A handful of rose petals
- A handful of lavender leaves/flowers
- A saucepan
- 1 bottle
- 2 cups of water
- A sieve

WHAT TO DO:

- Gently wash your rose petals, lavender leaves and flowers to remove any dirt.
- Add 2 cups of water to a saucepan and bring to the boil. Ask an adult to help you with this bit.
- Turn off the heat, add your petals to the water then leave to cool.
- Use a sieve to strain the contents away from the water and put the water in a pretty bottle.
- Think of a name for your perfume and decorate your bottle with a label and colourful ribbon.

MY BEAUTY ROUTINE

Month ....

BEAUTY FORECAST

What's on (parties / events / trips out)	When	Beauty buys & tries (I will try... I will buy...)
....	....	....
....	....	....
....	....	....
....	....	....
....	....	....

BEAUTY BESTIE

Describe the best beauty product you tried and tested this month.
Top beauty product: ....
It is perfect for my: ....

face ☐ body ☐ hair ☐

nails ☐ other ☐

Rate it: ☐ / 10

DRAW OR STICK A PIC OF IT HERE.

DID YOU KNOW?

It's official - perfume can make you feel better! Experts have linked scent to emotion, so try a lavender scent to help you relax or a lively citrus one for an instant energy boost.

MIRROR, MIRROR, ON THE WALL...

...who's the fairest of them all? Whose beauty style did you like this month? Draw or stick a pic of them here.

BEAUTY PASS-ON

What's the best beauty tip you heard this month?

....

....

I heard it from my...

friend..

sister..

mum..

gran..

other..

Best look on a friend was ....

....

My fave celeb look was ....

....

Don't forget the little extras to help you create the **WOW** factor!

INVENT YOUR OWN PERFUME...

What would it smell of..............................

Give it a name ....

Design a bottle for it here:

BEAUTY SLEEP

Everyone knows you feel better after a good night's sleep, but getting the right amount of sleep will help you look better too.

DREAM HOURS

When you're a baby, you need up to 18 hours of sleep a day. By the time you're a teenager, this has dropped to about nine hours. Sleep needs can vary from person to person, so it's important to recognize how much sleep YOU need to feel (and look) your best.

SEVEN STEPS TO SLEEP

Follow these simple steps to getting a good night's sleep:

1. Eat and drink well during the day and get plenty of sunshine and fresh air.
2. Eat your final meal at least three hours before you go to bed, so you don't go to sleep feeling too full or needing the loo.
3. Create a bedtime ritual: this could be a warm shower or bath, reading a book or listening to soothing music. These will then acts as triggers, telling your body sleep is on its way.
4. Take a tech-break from your computer and phone screen before your head hits the pillow. Writing a to-do list will also help de-clutter your mind.
5. Spray soothing scents around your room – lavender and jasmine are very relaxing.
6. Make sure your mattress is comfy and your bedroom dark and cool.
7. Try going to bed and getting up at the same time every day to regulate your body clock.

TURN TO PAGE 64 FOR SOME GREAT MAKES TO HELP YOU SLEEP.

BEAUTY-BOOSTING BENEFITS

Sleep is nature's most powerful beauty treatment.

When you're tired, your blood doesn't flow as effectively, which can deprive your cells of oxygen, stop cell growth and make your skin look dull. When you sleep, your skin renews itself and your facial muscles relax – so a good night's sleep helps your skin look softer and fresher.

DO!

Combine your beauty sleep routine with a sleepover and invite your friends round for an overnight pamper party!

SLEEPING BEAUTY

Night-time is the perfect time to pamper yourself, so try these overnight beauty tips and tricks while you sleep.

- Sleep on a satin pillow to reduce hair breakages and frizz.
- Braid your hair before you go to sleep and unravel it in the morning for natural waves.
- If your hair suffers from a serious lack of bounce, wash and dry it before bedtime and go to sleep in soft rollers. Just remember to take them out before you leave for school!
- Get rid of dry skin on your feet and hands by smothering them in moisturizing cream and going to sleep with gloves and socks on.
- Reduce dark under-eye circles (caused by fluid build up under the eye), by raising your head with a puffy pillow while you sleep.
- Apply any creams that contain brightening ingredients like retinol or vitamin C at night as sunlight can stop them working to their fullest potential.
- Sleeping on your back will enable your back and neck to rest in a natural position and improve your posture.

DO IT!

WHAT YOU NEED:

- Fabric 1 - 20 x 12cm
- Fabric 2 - 20 x 12cm
- Black felt - 20 x 12cm
- Length of elastic
- Scissors
- Needle and thread
- Template - look!

SWEET DREAMS

Try these great makes to help you snooze in style.

1.

SLEEP MASK

If counting sheep isn't working, slip on this black-out sleep mask for a perfect night's sleep.

2.

3.

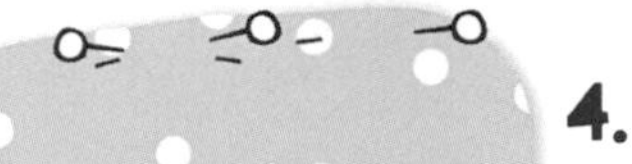

4.

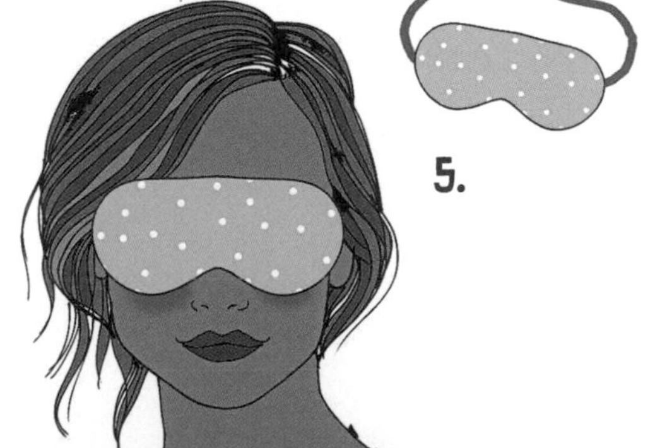

5.

WHAT TO DO:

- Copy the sleep-mask pattern above and cut it out to create a template. You'll need to make it a bit larger to cover your eyes.
- Use your template to cut out one piece of outer fabric and one piece of reverse fabric. Then cut out a slightly smaller piece of felt.
- Pin your fabrics together, so the pretty side of fabrics 1 and 2 are facing each other and sew the edges together. Leave one of the shorter sides unsewn.
- Turn the mask inside out and insert the black felt lining. Then pin the remaining edges together and neatly sew up.
- To finish, remove the pins and sew a length of elastic to either side of the mask and you'll be ready to snuggle down and catch some zzzzzzs!

LAVENDER BAG

Sweet dreams are guaranteed when you pop this lavender bag inside your pillowcase.

WHAT YOU NEED:

- 2 x fabric pieces 10 x 15cm
- 15cm ribbon
- 1 x bunch of dried lavender
- Scissors
- Needle and thread

WHAT TO DO:

1. Remove the flowers from your dried lavender.

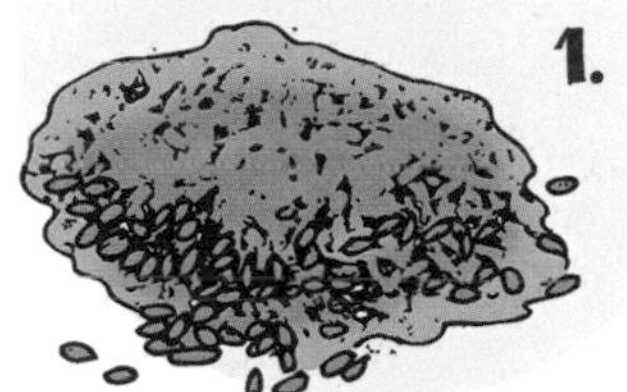

2. Pin your fabric pieces so the pretty sides are facing each other.

3. Sew the fabrics together along the two longer sides and shorter bottom side, to create a sachet bag, leaving the top open.

4. Turn the sachet bag right side out and carefully spoon your lavender into it.

5. Tie a length of ribbon around the top opening, to close it.

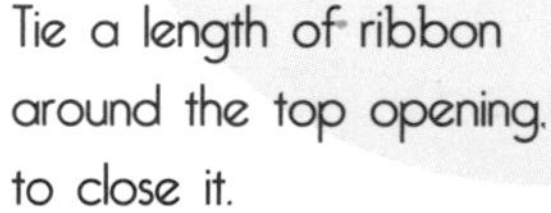

MY BEAUTY ROUTINE

Month ....

BEAUTY FORECAST

What's on (parties / events / trips out)	When	Beauty buys & tries (I will try... I will buy...)
....	....	....
....	....	....
....	....	....
....	....	....
....	....	....

BEAUTY BESTIE

Describe the best beauty product you tried and tested this month.

Top beauty product: ....

It is perfect for my: ....

face ☐ body ☐ hair ☐

nails ☐ other ☐

Rate it: ☐ / 10

DRAW OR STICK A PIC OF IT HERE.

DID YOU KNOW?

If it takes you less than five minutes to fall asleep at night you might be sleep deprived as it should take around ten minutes.

Don't forget the little extras to help you create the **WOW** factor!

Design some cool sunglasses to finish off your look.

Doodle a bangle you'd like to wear in the box below.

DREAM DECODER

Work out what your dreams mean with the chart below.

FALLING DREAMS

If you dream you are falling, either from the sky or from a cliff or down a hole, this can mean you feel out of control. Try to work out what area of your life you need to take control of and what you can do and these dreams should stop.

DREAMING THAT YOU CAN'T TALK

Dreaming you can't speak can often mean you are afraid to tell people what you think and to voice your true opinions. A good way to solve this problem is by writing down your thoughts, then slowly, over time, you should build up the courage to say what you think.

FLYING DREAMS

Dreaming of flying means you are feeling confident and secure about your life and totally in control. If you worry that you are flying too high in your dream, it sometimes means you are worried about how your success will change you and your life.

PICTURE PERFECT

DO IT!

Now that you've got your beauty look all sorted - make sure you take some awesome pics of yourself to share with your friends and family.

HOW TO TAKE A GREAT SELFIE:

Follow these simple rules to getting the best shot.

1. Download a photo app on your phone that will help you create your masterpiece.

2. Choose a favourite outfit that you feel comfortable in. If you feel good, you'll look good!

3. Make sure you get the light right by stepping outside. Early morning or late afternoon is the best time to take your pic.

4. Pick your location and check out what's behind you - you don't want anyone or anything photo-bombing you!

5. Don't pout - just smile naturally. Be brave and show your teeth.

6. Either look directly at your phone/camera or look elsewhere and pretend you're having a conversation with someone, even if no one else is around.

THAT'S IT – YOU'RE DONE!

POSING TIPS AND TRICKS

Whether you're taking the shot or posing for a snap - check out what to do and why. You'll then take great pics of you and your friends.

DO! Practise your pose in front of a mirror.

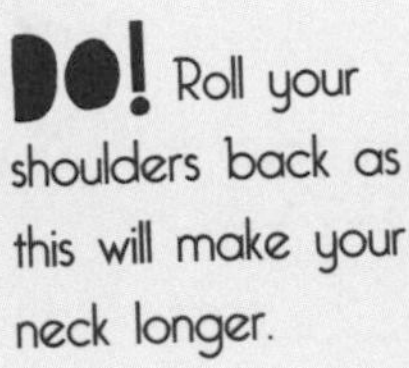

DO! Roll your shoulders back as this will make your neck longer.

DO! Take your camera or phone everywhere. Practice makes perfect and the more photos you take, the better your pics will be.

DO! Position your arms away from your body and rest your hands on your hips - this will make you look relaxed and natural.

DON'T! Wear heavily patterned clothes. Keep it plain and simple so your face stands out, not your clothes.

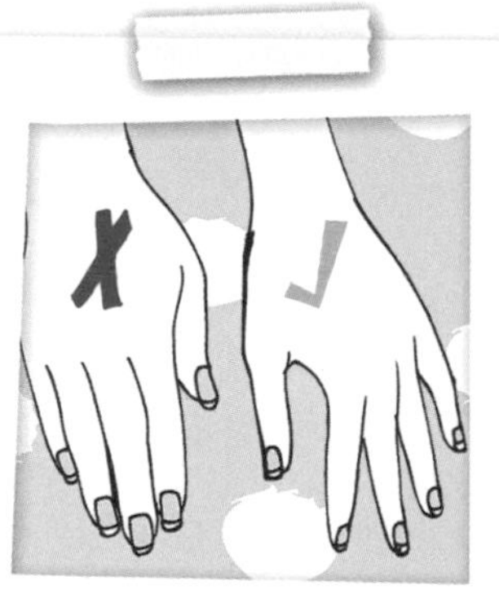

DON'T! Clump your fingers together as this will make your hands look big.

DON'T! Forget the little things. A dirty mark or a tangled necklace can ruin a shot.

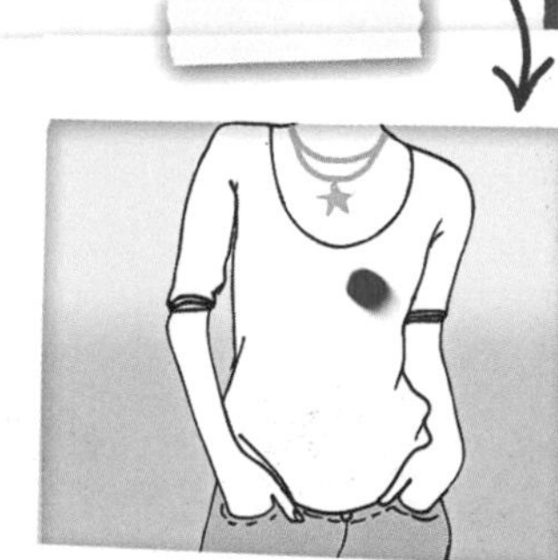

MY BEAUTY ROUTINE

Month ....

BEAUTY FORECAST

What's on (parties / events / trips out)	When	Beauty buys & tries (I will try... I will buy...)
....	....	....
....	....	....
....	....	....
....	....	....
....	....	....

BEAUTY BESTIE

Describe the best beauty product you tried and tested this month.

Top beauty product: ....

It is perfect for my: ....

face ☐ body ☐ hair ☐

nails ☐ other ☐

Rate it: ☐ / 10

DRAW OR STICK A PIC OF IT HERE.

DID YOU KNOW?

One of the most expensive beauty treatments in the world is a gold-leaf facial, where pieces of gold are rubbed into the skin to improve the complexion.

TIMELESS BEAUTY

Does your beauty routine run like clockwork, or is it a bit more random? Fill in the chart below to get the low-down on your beauty habits.

How often do you...	Twice a day	Every day	Once a week	Twice a week	Once a month	Never	Other
Wash your hair?							
Brush your teeth?							
Get a haircut?							
File your nails?							
Paint your nails?							
Exfoliate?							

PERFECT PICS

Stick your best selfies and pics of friends here.

BEAUTY ROUND-UP

It's official - you are now a beauty expert! Fill in the page with your best beauty tips, tricks, buys and tries...

My fave hairstyle looks like this...

MY TOP THREE BEAUTY BESTIES

1. ....
....
2. ....
....
3. ....
....

MY TOP THREE ACCESSORIES

1. ....
....
2. ....
....
3. ....
....

Colour in the face to show your fave eye shadow, blusher and lipstick colours.

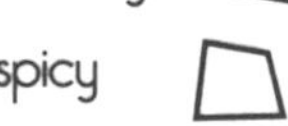

Number these scents from 1 to 3, in order of preference...

fruity ☐
flowery ☐
spicy ☐

TECHNICAL TERMS

ANTIOXIDANTS A substance, such as vitamins A, C and E, that slows down the damage formed by environmental hazards, like air pollution and pesticides.

CUTICLES An outer layer of harder skin around the nail bed.

DANDRUFF White-ish flakes of dead skin that appear on the scalp and in the hair.

ENDORPHINS Natural chemicals in the body that fight pain. Endorphins are released by the body when a person gets hurt, but also during exercise and laughter.

EXFOLIATE To gently brush away dead skin cells on the body to improve the appearance of the skin.

FOLLICLES A bit like a small tube in the skin where the hair grows and pushes out through the skin. If you have straight hair, your follicles are perfectly round. If you have curly hair your follicles are more oval shaped, and the flatter the oval, the curlier the hair.

TOOLS OF THE TRADE

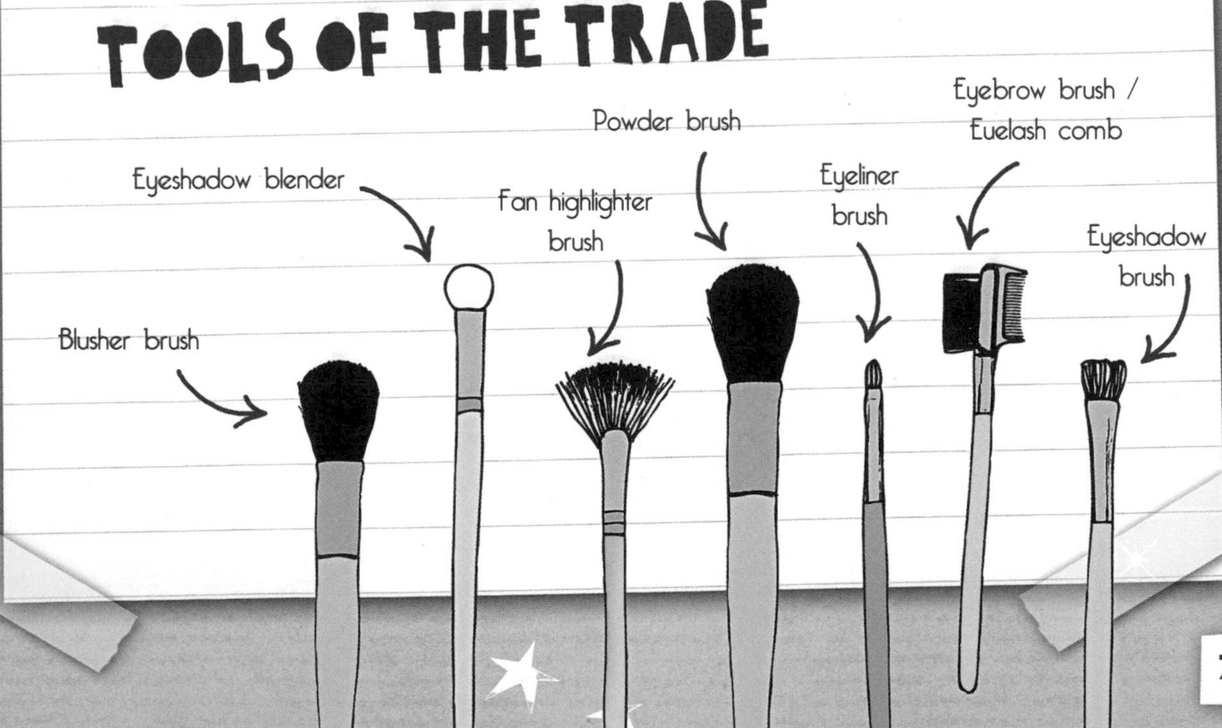

FASHION
"Style is a way to say who you are without having to speak."
- Rachel Zoe

LOOK OF THE MONTH

"Look of the Month" pages are a chance for you to record and design your own fabulous looks and to devise finishing touches that will make them even more stylish.

CREATE the perfect look here, either by drawing or sticking pictures onto the mannequin, or by creating and using some fashion stencils.

Use this space to **DESIGN** some cool accessories and add the finishing touches to your look.

Improve your **FASHION KNOW-HOW** with these fun fashion facts.

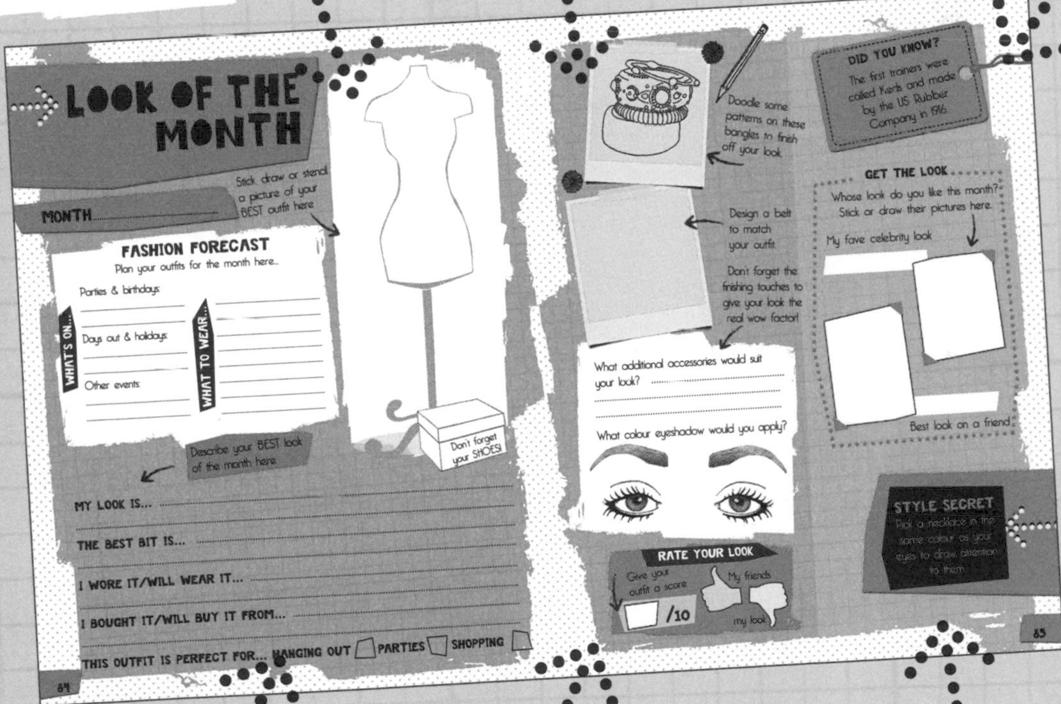

WHAT'S GOING ON THIS MONTH? Use this section to write down what events you have coming up and, more importantly, what you plan to wear to them.

RATE YOUR LOOK here and find out what your mates thought of it, too.

Keep an eye out for these great little **STYLE SECRETS**, giving you the lowdown on how to make a great look even better!

STEAL THE STYLE

"Steal the Style" pages focus on all the different fashion trends, from animal print and denim to festival chic and sports luxe. Packed with style tips and tricks, you're sure to find the perfect look for you.

Find out how to **WEAR IT WELL** with tips and tricks on how to work the style into your wardrobe and life.

From fun quizzes to find out what will suit you best to great ways to transform your wardrobe – these pages are over-flowing with useful information on how to **GET THE LOOK**.

STEAL THE STYLE

ANIMAL PRINT

Take a walk on the wild side and introduce some animal prints into your wardrobe.

WEAR IT WELL...

Follow these fashion rules for a purrrrfect look every time.

1 Add a leopard-skin handbag or scarf to an everyday outfit for an instant animal fashion fix.

2 Stand out from the crowd in bright neon-coloured animal prints, or play it safe with neutral and earthy tones.

3 Tone down a loud animal print and steal some of its attention by teaming it with a vibrant colour.

4 Use a snakeskin-look belt to add texture and glamour to a casual outfit.

5 Animal-print shoes are a great way to stay on trend and they look great with jeans and black trousers.

SPOT THE DIFFERENCE

There are all kinds of animal prints to choose from, but do you know your cheetah from your leopard print, and which one is your favourite? Rate the patterns below – 1 for the best and 5 for the worst.

SNAKESKIN

ZEBRA

LEOPARD

CHEETAH

CROCODILE

86

ANIMAL MAGIC

Show off your styling skills by creating some animal-print outfits.

Draw lines to show which items you'd wear together.

FEATHERY FASHION

For a more delicate approach to this style, opt for clothes with a pretty bird, butterfly or stylish feather pattern. Turn to page 22 to create your own animal-pattern stencil to use on your clothes.

DO! Experiment with colour. There are some amazing coloured animal-prints so don't be afraid to try them.

DON'T! Mix your animal-prints. Stick to one animal pattern at a time.

87

All aspects of the style are covered, from **CLOTHES** and **SHOES** to **ACCESSORIES** and **HAIRSTYLES**.

Check out these fashion **DOs** and **DON'Ts** to ensure you nail the look.

Crafty fashionistas will love all the great makes, from quick and easy ways to transform a t-shirt and how to make a handbag, to simple sewing and embroidery tips.

Look out for the different **SKILL LEVELS**. One scissor means a quick and easy make, two scissors will take a bit longer, and three means you'll need lots of tools and time! ✂✂✂

Make it! COLLAR NECKLACE

Create your own collar necklace – guaranteed to make the simplest of tops look super stylish

TOOLS: A4 sheet of paper, pencil, pins, scissors, a piece of material (approx 20 x 28 cm), 90 cm of thin ribbon (cut into 3 x 30 cm lengths), sequins, glue
TIME: 15 mins **SKILL LEVEL:** ✂✂

★ First, draw a paper pattern of two identical collar shapes for your necklace. Cut them out and test them against one of your t-shirts or tops to make sure they are a good fit.

★ Next, pin your collar patterns to your chosen material and cut around them.

Tip: you can use any material you like. Choose a colour that will go with lots of your tops and if you don't want to buy any material, recycle something you have already, like an old pillowcase.

★ Snip two small holes in either end of both your collar shapes.

★ Join the collar shapes together at the front by threading one of your pieces of thin ribbon through the inside holes and tying a simple knot or bow.

★ Thread the two remaining lengths of thin ribbon through each of the outside holes and secure with a small knot. Hold the collar up to your neck and check the ribbons are long enough to reach around your neck and tie in a bow.

★ For a sparkly finish stick some pretty sequins along the edge of the collar shapes.

DID YOU KNOW?
Collar necklaces have been fashionable for thousands of years. Ancient Egyptians made them from rows and rows of coloured beads.

Tip: for a different look, use stickers or card buttons to finish off your necklace.

88 89

Make it! pages show you how to create a unique and stylish fashion item.

How to pages will teach you a fashion skill like embroidery or stencilling.

Make it! HOW TO EMBROIDER

Customise your clothes with cute embroidery patches

TOOLS: tracing paper, pencil, fabric swatch approx 10 cm x 10 cm, needle, threads, scissors **TIME:** approx 30 mins to 1 hour **SKILL LEVEL:** ✂✂

Make your own patches with one of these patterns, or design your own.

How To Make Your Patch

★ Pick an embroidery pattern below and trace over it using a pencil and tracing paper.

★ Lay your tracing paper face down onto your fabric swatch and draw firmly over the shape to transfer the pencil marks onto the fabric.

★ Stitch over your pencil marks with your chosen coloured threads.

How To Sew

Sewing and embroidery are useful skills for customizing clothes. If you don't know how, here are the basics.

★ Pass a length of thread through the eye (hole) in your needle (A) and tie a knot at the end to secure (B).

SATIN STITCH
A satin stitch allows you to decorate a simple pattern.
★ Sew straight parallel stitches across the shape or pattern you are making.

RUNNING STITCH
A running stitch is the most straightforward embroidery stitch and easy to learn and use.
★ Push the needle back and forth through your fabric at equal points for a neat stitch that will hold your fabric together or create a pretty pattern.

Uniquely Yours

You can use your embroidered patches to customize your clothes and accessories. Sew them on to re-invent old favourites from your jeans, t-shirt and gloves to a bag or pencil case.

DO!
For a more professional finish stitch through two layers of fabric instead of one, so you can't see through the fabric to any knots and tangles at the back.

130 131

Make it! TRANSFORM A T-SHIRT!

Fed up of your boring old white t-shirt? Check out these crafty ways to give it the ultimate makeover.

super speedy

1 **TOOLS:** scissors
TIME: 5 mins **SKILL LEVEL:** ✂
Cut the sleeves and collar off and turn your t-shirt into a vest.

Tip: chop a couple of cms off the bottom if you want to turn it into a crop top.

perfect patch

2 **TOOLS:** applique patches, an iron **TIME:** 15 mins
SKILL LEVEL: ✂✂
Iron applique patches like pretty hearts, butterflies and flowers onto the t-shirt for a fun and stylish look.

DO!
Ask a grown-up to help you with the iron.

bags of fun

3 **TOOLS:** scissors, needle, thread
TIME: 20 mins
SKILL LEVEL: ✂✂
Transform your t-shirt into a cool bag. Snip off the collar and sleeves and stitch up the bottom of the t-shirt.

Tip: decorate your bag using stencils and applique patches.

makeover magic

4 **TOOLS:** scissors, needle, thread
TIME: 20 mins **SKILL LEVEL:** ✂✂
Convert your t-shirt into a skirt. Cut off the neckline so it's wide enough to fit around your waist. Sew up the sleeves and poke them inside the t-shirt so they become the skirt's pockets.

Tip: use some ribbon or a belt to stylishly hold the skirt in place.

stencil style

5 **TOOLS:** stencils, fabric pens, paint **TIME:** 20 mins
SKILL LEVEL: ✂✂
If drawing isn't your strong point, use the stencils included with the book to create a cool pattern or picture on your t-shirt.

new look

6 **TOOLS:** pencil, ruler, scissors, ribbon
TIME: 30 mins **SKILL LEVEL:** ✂✂✂
For a stylish transformation cut across the neckline of your t-shirt to get rid of the collar. Then, using a ruler and pencil, mark out two rows of dots about 3 cm apart down the back of your t-shirt and cut small holes where the dots are. Attach a safety pin to your ribbon and thread it through the holes as if you are lacing up a shoe. Tie a bow at the end of the ribbon to secure.

Tip: change your ribbon to match your outfit.

DID YOU KNOW?

82 83

Transform pages help you turn old clothes into something fresh and new.

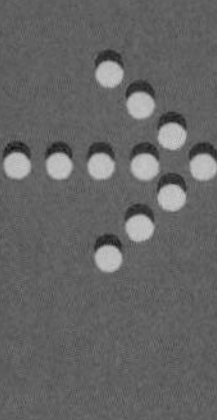

LOOK OF THE MONTH

MONTH..

Stick, draw or stencil a picture of your BEST outfit here

FASHION FORECAST

Plan your outfits for the month here...

WHAT'S ON...

Parties & birthdays:

....

....

Days out & holidays:

....

....

Other events:

....

....

WHAT TO WEAR...

....

....

....

....

....

....

....

....

Don't forget your SHOES!

Describe your BEST look of the month here

MY LOOK IS... ....

....

THE BEST BIT IS... ....

....

I WORE IT/WILL WEAR IT... ....

....

I BOUGHT IT/WILL BUY IT FROM... ....

....

THIS OUTFIT IS PERFECT FOR... HANGING OUT 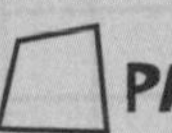 **PARTIES**  **SHOPPING** ☐

Create a hairstyle to go with your look

Add some cool accessories to finish off your look

Don't forget the finishing touches to give your look the real wow factor!

What coat did you/would you pick for your look and why?

....

....

Create a trendy design for your nails.

RATE YOUR LOOK

Give your outfit a score

/10

My friends

my look

DID YOU KNOW?

Before the 19th century, there were no fashion models and designers had to use dolls to display their creations.

GET THE LOOK

Whose look do you like this month? Stick or draw their pictures here.

My fave celebrity look

Best look on a friend

STYLE SECRET

Go for a look that suits you and your personality. You won't look good if you don't feel good.

STEAL THE STYLE

DENIM

Denim is every girl's best fashion friend. Dress it up or dress it down for a perfect look every time.

WEAR IT WELL...

Follow these simple rules to get the most out of your denim...

1 Team denim skirts with loose-fitting hoody tops or t-shirts for a cool casual look.

2 Try high-waisted jeans for longer looking legs.

3 For a groovy retro look opt for bell-bottom or flared jeans.

4 For a stylish contrast, dress down a frilly dress or a girly skirt with a denim jacket.

5 Try to avoid top-to-toe denim – it only looks good on cowboys!

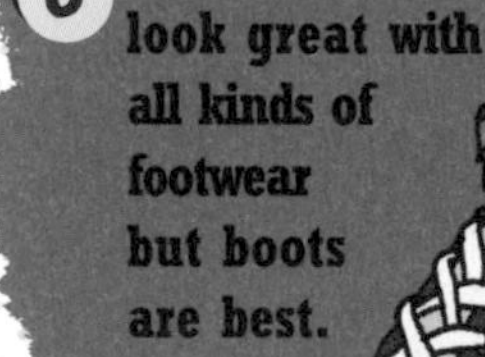

6 Skinny jeans look great with all kinds of footwear but boots are best.

7 Always buy jeans that are slightly tight as they stretch every time you wear them.

8 Wear denim shorts all year round by layering them over leggings when it gets cold.

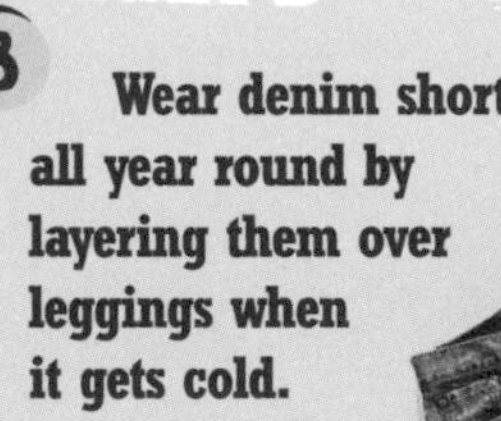

JEAN-IUS INVENTION

1872
Jacob Davis and Levi Strauss created the first jeans or "waist overalls" for workers and miners.

1934
The first pair of women's jeans were called "Lady Levi's" and designed for women who worked on ranches.

1950
Jeans gained cult status when actors wore them in the movies and teenagers wore them as a sign of rebellion.

TODAY
everyone wears jeans from pop stars to pets!

TRUE BLUE

Denim comes in loads of cool shades. Which is your favourite?

FADED

BLUE

ACID

INDIGO

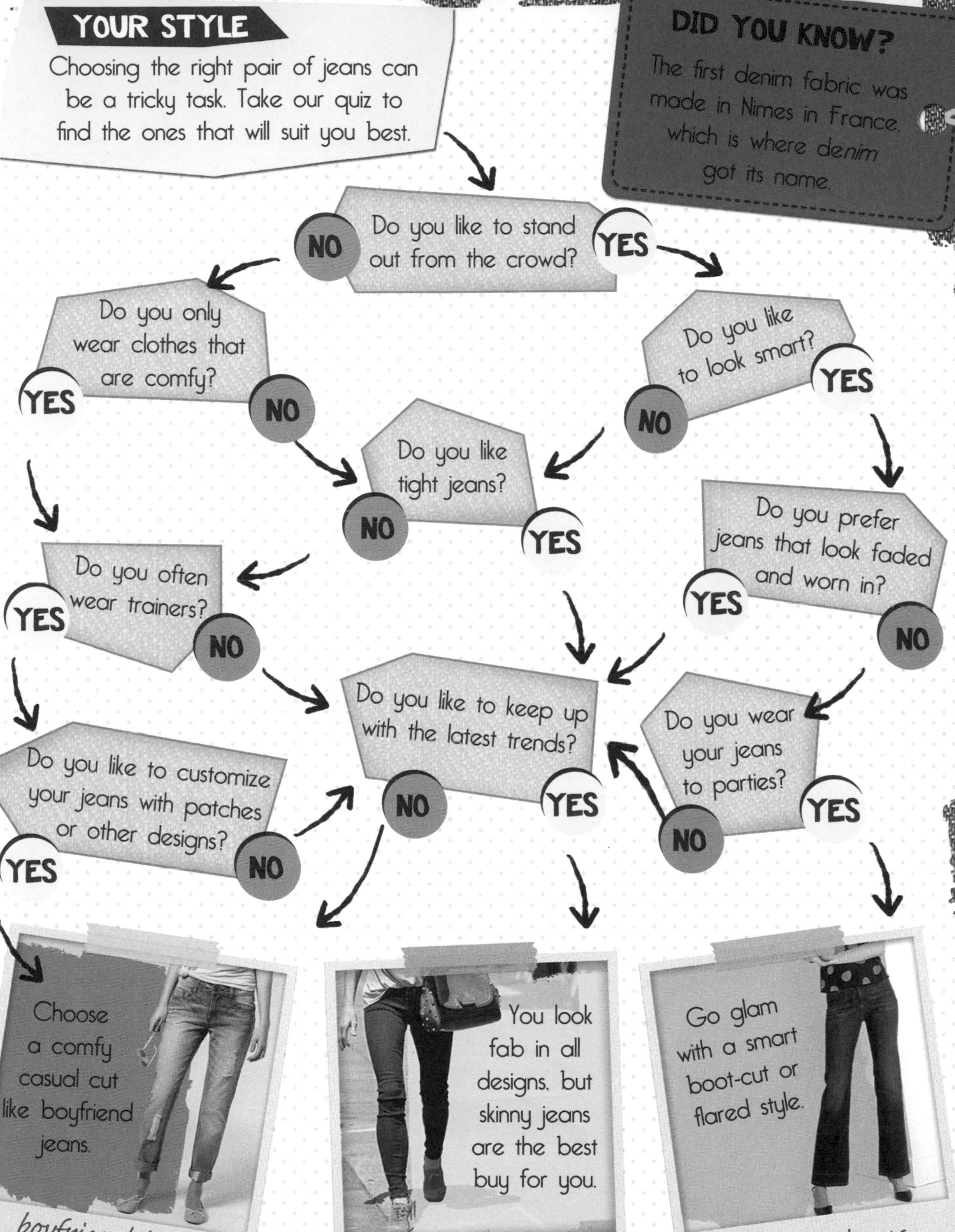
YOUR STYLE
Choosing the right pair of jeans can be a tricky task. Take our quiz to find the ones that will suit you best.
DID YOU KNOW?
The first denim fabric was made in Nimes in France, which is where *denim* got its name.
Do you like to stand out from the crowd?
NO
YES
Do you only wear clothes that are comfy?
YES
NO
Do you like to look smart?
NO
YES
Do you like tight jeans?
NO
YES
Do you prefer jeans that look faded and worn in?
YES
NO
Do you often wear trainers?
YES
NO
Do you like to keep up with the latest trends?
NO
YES
Do you wear your jeans to parties?
NO
YES
Do you like to customize your jeans with patches or other designs?
YES
NO
Choose a comfy casual cut like boyfriend jeans.
boyfriend jeans
You look fab in all designs, but skinny jeans are the best buy for you.
skinny jeans
Go glam with a smart boot-cut or flared style.
boot-cut jeans

Make it!

TRANSFORM A T-SHIRT!

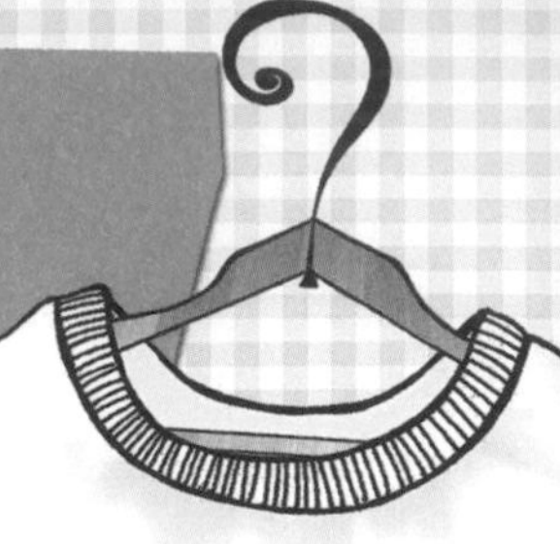

Fed up of your boring old white t-shirt? Check out these crafty ways to give it the ultimate makeover.

Super speedy

1 TOOLS: scissors
TIME: 5 mins **SKILL LEVEL:** ✂

Cut the sleeves and collar off and turn your t-shirt into a vest.

Tip: chop a couple of cms off the bottom if you want to turn it into a crop top.

Perfect patch

2 TOOLS: applique patches, an iron **TIME:** 15 mins
SKILL LEVEL: ✂✂

Iron applique patches like pretty hearts, butterflies and flowers onto the t-shirt for a fun and stylish look.

DO!
Ask a grown-up to help you with the iron.

Bags of fun

3 TOOLS: scissors, needle, thread
TIME: 20 mins
SKILL LEVEL: ✂✂

Transform your t-shirt into a cool bag. Snip off the collar and sleeves and stitch up the bottom of the t-shirt.

Tip: decorate your bag using stencils and applique patches.

Makeover magic

4 **TOOLS:** scissors, needle, thread
TIME: 20 mins **SKILL LEVEL:** ✂✂

Convert your t-shirt into a skirt. Cut off the neckline so it's wide enough to fit around your waist. Sew up the sleeves and poke them inside the t-shirt so they become the skirt's pockets.

Tip: use some ribbon or a belt to stylishly hold the skirt in place.

Stencil style

5 **TOOLS:** stencils, fabric pens, paint **TIME:** 20 mins
SKILL LEVEL: ✂✂

If drawing isn't your strong point, make or print off some stencils to create a cool pattern or picture on your t-shirt.

New look

6 **TOOLS:** pencil, ruler, scissors, ribbon
TIME: 30 mins **SKILL LEVEL:** ✂✂✂

For a stylish transformation cut across the neckline of your t-shirt to get rid of the collar. Then, using a ruler and pencil, mark out two rows of dots about 3 cm apart down the back of your t-shirt and cut small holes where the dots are. Attach a safety pin to your ribbon and thread it through the holes as if you are lacing up a shoe. Tie a bow at the end of the ribbon to secure.

Tip: change your ribbon to match your outfit.

DID YOU KNOW?
2 billion t-shirts are sold worldwide each year!

LOOK OF THE MONTH

MONTH...

Stick, draw or stencil a picture of your BEST outfit here

FASHION FORECAST

Plan your outfits for the month here...

WHAT'S ON...

Parties & birthdays:

....

....

Days out & holidays:

....

....

Other events:

....

....

WHAT TO WEAR...

....

....

....

....

....

....

....

....

Don't forget your SHOES!

Describe your BEST look of the month here

MY LOOK IS... ....

....

THE BEST BIT IS... ....

....

I WORE IT/WILL WEAR IT... ....

....

I BOUGHT IT/WILL BUY IT FROM... ....

....

THIS OUTFIT IS PERFECT FOR... HANGING OUT ☐ **PARTIES** ☐ **SHOPPING** ☐

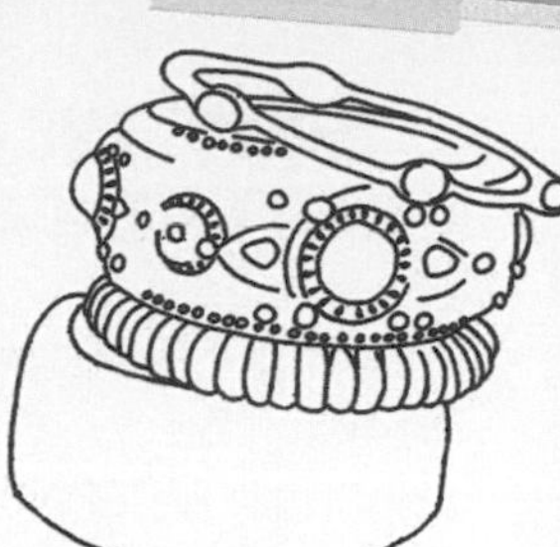

Doodle some patterns on these bangles to finish off your look.

Design a belt to match your outfit.

Don't forget the finishing touches to give your look the real wow factor!

What additional accessories would suit your look? ....

....

....

What colour eyeshadow would you apply?

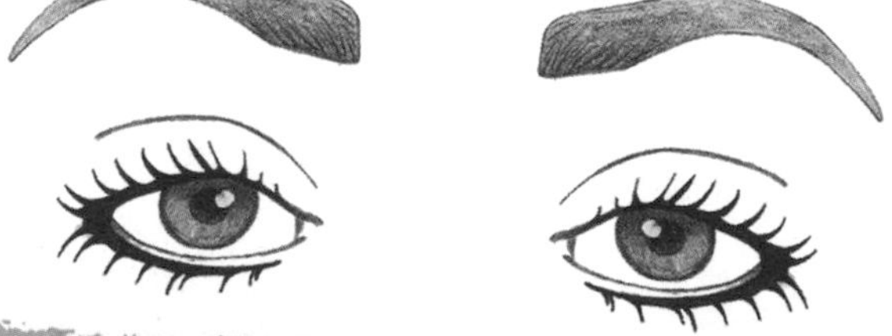

RATE YOUR LOOK

Give your outfit a score

/10

My friends

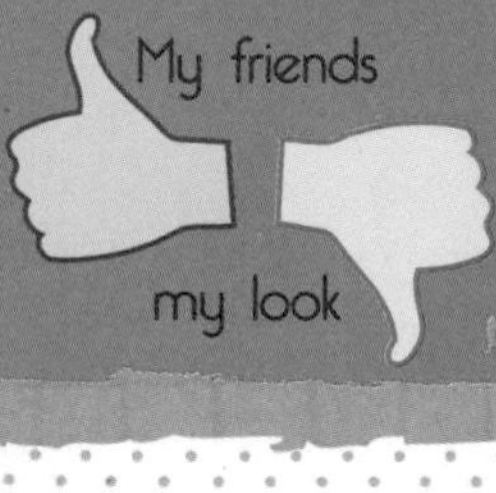

my look

DID YOU KNOW?

The first trainers were called Keds and made by the US Rubber Company in 1916.

GET THE LOOK

Whose look do you like this month? Stick or draw their pictures here.

STYLE SECRET

Pick a necklace in the same colour as your eyes to draw attention to them.

STEAL THE STYLE

ANIMAL PRINT

Take a walk on the wild side and introduce some animal prints into your wardrobe.

WEAR IT WELL...

Follow these fashion rules for a purrrrfect look every time.

1 **Add a leopard-skin handbag or scarf to an everyday outfit for an instant animal fashion fix.**

2 **Stand out from the crowd in bright neon-coloured animal prints, or play it safe with neutral and earthy tones.**

3 **Use a snakeskin-look belt to add texture and glamour to a casual outfit.**

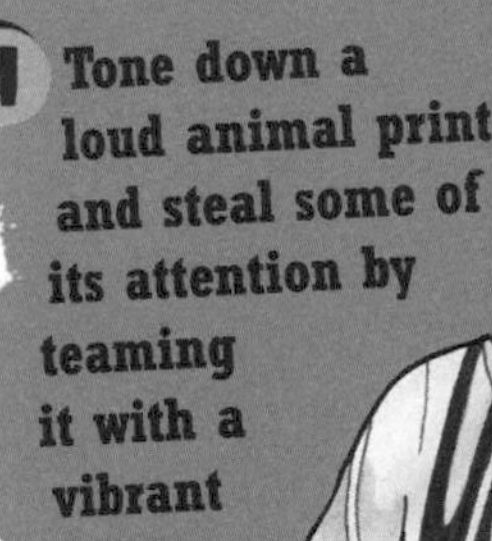

4 **Tone down a loud animal print and steal some of its attention by teaming it with a vibrant colour.**

5 **Animal-print shoes are a great way to stay on trend and they look great with jeans and black trousers.**

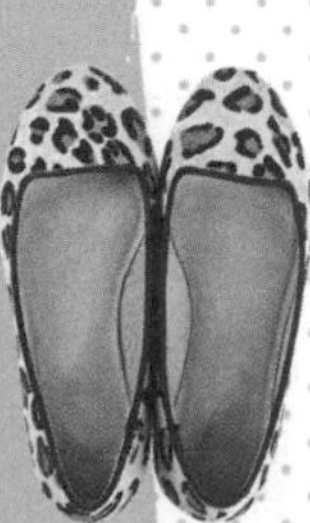

SPOT THE DIFFERENCE

There are all kinds of animal prints to choose from, but do you know your cheetah from your leopard print, and which one is your favourite?

Rate the patterns below – 1 for the best and 5 for the worst.

SNAKESKIN

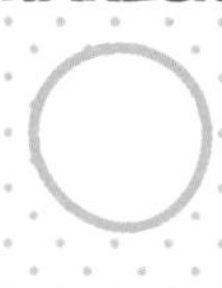

ZEBRA

LEOPARD

CHEETAH

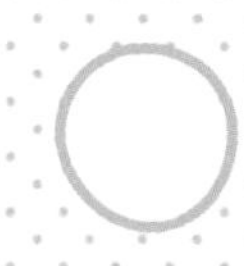

CROCODILE

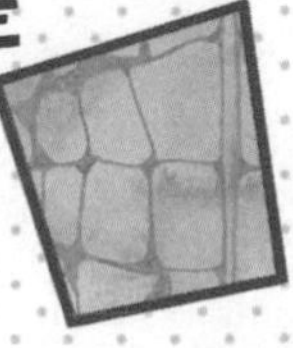

ANIMAL MAGIC

Show off your styling skills by creating some animal-print outfits.

Draw lines to show which items you'd wear together.

FEATHERY FASHION

For a more delicate approach to this style, opt for clothes with a pretty bird, butterfly or stylish feather pattern. You can create your own animal-pattern stencil to use on your clothes.

DO! Experiment with colour. There are some amazing coloured animal prints so don't be afraid to try them.

DON'T! Mix your animal prints. Stick to one animal pattern at a time.

Make it!

COLLAR NECKLACE

Create your own collar necklace - guaranteed to make the simplest of tops look super stylish.

TOOLS: A4 sheet of paper, pencil, pins, scissors, a piece of material approx. 20 x 28 cm, 90 cm of thin ribbon cut into 3 x 30 cm lengths, sequins, glue

TIME: 15 mins

SKILL LEVEL: ✂✂

★ First, draw a paper pattern of two identical collar shapes for your necklace. Cut them out and test them against one of your t-shirts or tops to make sure they are a good fit.

★ Next, pin your collar patterns to your chosen material and cut around them.

Tip: you can use any material you like. Choose a colour that will go with lots of your tops. If you don't want to buy any material, recycle something you have already, like an old pillowcase.

★ Snip two small holes in either end of both your collar shapes.

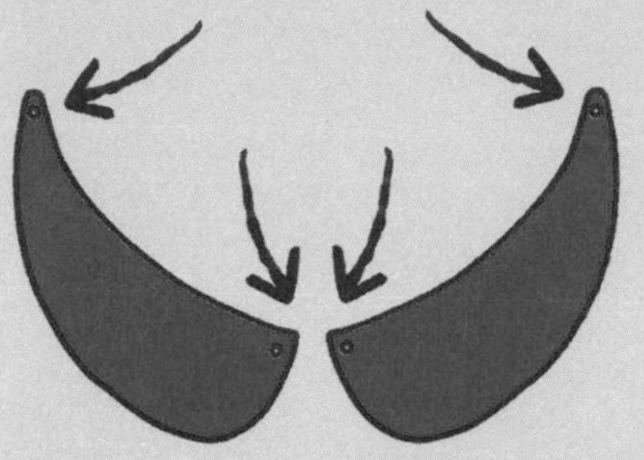

★ Join the collar shapes together at the front by threading one of your pieces of thin ribbon through the inside holes and tying a simple knot or bow.

★ Thread the two remaining lengths of thin ribbon through each of the outside holes and secure with a small knot. Hold the collar up to your neck and check that the ribbons are long enough to reach around your neck and tie in a bow.

★ For a sparkly finish, stick some pretty sequins along the edge of the collar shapes.

DID YOU KNOW?

Collar necklaces have been fashionable for thousands of years. Ancient Egyptians made theirs from rows and rows of coloured beads.

Tip: for a different look, use stickers or buttons to finish off your necklace.

MONTH...

Stick, draw or stencil a picture of your BEST outfit here

FASHION FORECAST

Plan your outfits for the month here...

WHAT'S ON...

Parties & birthdays:

....

....

Days out & holidays:

....

....

Other events:

....

....

WHAT TO WEAR...

....

....

....

....

....

....

....

....

Don't forget your SHOES!

Describe your BEST look of the month here

MY LOOK IS... ....

....

THE BEST BIT IS... ....

....

I WORE IT/WILL WEAR IT... ....

....

I BOUGHT IT/WILL BUY IT FROM... ....

....

THIS OUTFIT IS PERFECT FOR... HANGING OUT ☐ **PARTIES**  **SHOPPING** 

Draw a handbag to go with your outfit.
Add a cool scarf to finish off your look.
Don't forget the finishing touches to give your look the real wow factor!
Which shoes did you choose for this look and why?
What kind of earrings would suit your look? Draw them here.
RATE YOUR LOOK
Give your outfit a score
/10
My friends
my look
DID YOU KNOW?
Vintage clothing dates from 1920 to 1960. Anything made after this time is considered retro.
GET THE LOOK
Whose look do you like this month? Stick or draw their pictures here.
My fave celebrity look
Best look on a friend
STYLE SECRET
If you like wearing neutral colours, brighten up your outfits with bold and patterned accessories.

STEAL THE STYLE

SPORTS STAR

Look like a winner in a cool and casual sporty style.

WEAR IT WELL...

Check out these fashion guidelines for a sporty look bursting with energy.

1 **Trainers are a fashion must-have for this style. Keep on trend with some wedge high-tops or opt for classic pumps.**

2 **Try a cropped or lace-fronted jumper for a stylish twist on a sporty fashion favourite.**

3 **Cosy and comfy, a hoodie looks good with everything. Wear it with a short denim skirt, over a dress or with your favourite pair of jeans.**

4 **Cute skater dresses, inspired by ice-skating costumes, look great all year round. Wear with ballet pumps when it's warm or over leggings when the temperature drops.**

5 **Get the look on top with a baseball cap or cosy beanie hat. For a more retro sporty style, try a sun visor.**

SPORTS LUXE

Sportswear designs in exciting textures and colours are a winning combination on the catwalk. Look out for high-street versions of the designer trends, from block colours and neon dresses, to trousers with go-faster stripes, tops with chevrons and metallic trainers.

DID YOU KNOW?

Tennis player Suzanne Lenglen shocked the world in 1922 when she appeared at the Wimbledon tennis tournament in a short skirt and short sleeves. It was the first time a woman had played in such an outfit, but others soon followed.

WHATS YOUR STYLE?

There are so many great sporty styles, it's hard to know which one will suit you best. Take this quiz to find your winning look.

	YES	NO
You like wearing dresses.	☐	☐
You prefer shoes to trainers.	☐	☐
You love mixing and matching different colours and styles.	☐	☐
You always make time to accessorize.	☐	☐
You like to try out all the new fashions.	☐	☐

MOSTLY YES

You like to experiment to get your outfit just right. Try new fashion trends, like skater dresses and sportswear, in different fabrics and colours for a medal-winning look.

MOSTLY NO

Comfort is key for you - stick to safe sporty styles like jeans, hoodies and trainers and you'll not only look good but you'll feel great too.

Get the look in one easy step with a cool, sporty varsity jacket. The casual design looks great over t-shirts with jeans. For a bit of sports luxe, pick one in a bright colour or silky fabric.

DANCING SPIRIT

Ballet fashion isn't all tutus and tiaras, it's also a great way to create a prettier and more delicate sporty look. Think pink and wear wrap-over cardigans, leotard tops and ballet pumps. For an edgier style opt for legwarmers over your jeans.

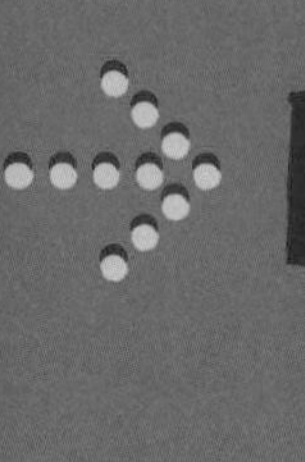

LOOK OF THE MONTH

MONTH..

Stick, draw or stencil a picture of your BEST outfit here

FASHION FORECAST

Plan your outfits for the month here...

WHAT'S ON...

Parties & birthdays:

....

....

Days out & holidays:

....

....

Other events:

....

....

WHAT TO WEAR...

....

....

....

....

....

....

....

....

Don't forget your SHOES!

Describe your BEST look of the month here

MY LOOK IS... ....

....

THE BEST BIT IS... ....

....

I WORE IT/WILL WEAR IT... ....

....

I BOUGHT IT/WILL BUY IT FROM... ....

....

THIS OUTFIT IS PERFECT FOR... HANGING OUT ☐ PARTIES ☐ SHOPPING ☐

Design some cool sunglasses to finish off your look.

Accessorize your outfit with some sparkly jewellery.

Don't forget the finishing touches to give your look the real wow factor!

Which hairstyle did you pick and why?

....

....

What colour lip gloss did you/ would you use? Create the perfect pout here.

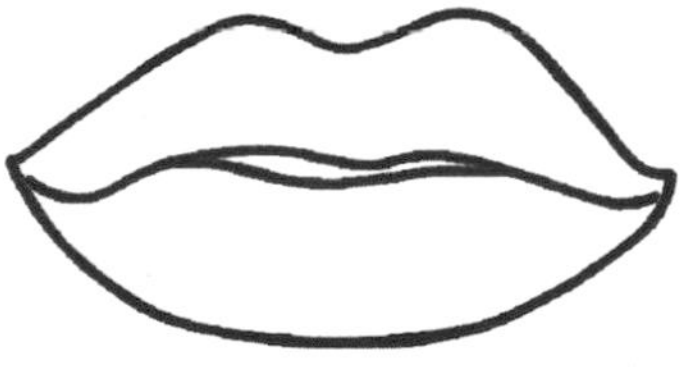

RATE YOUR LOOK

Give your outfit a score

/10

My friends

my look

DID YOU KNOW?

During the Renaissance period, around the 1500s, it was fashionable to shave your eyebrows off. Today, it's fashionable to darken and define eyebrows with an eyebrow pencil.

GET THE LOOK

Whose look do you like this month? Stick or draw their pictures here.

My fave celebrity look

Best look on a friend

STYLE SECRET

Add different buttons to a jacket or cardigan to give it a unique style.

STEAL THE STYLE

BEACH BABE

Show off your sunny side with the hottest beach fashions and the coolest accessories.

BEACH BLING

Choose jewellery with a seashore theme, from bracelets with rope knots to coloured pearl necklaces and pretty starfish earrings. Anklets and toe rings look great on the beach – paint your toes in a pretty pastel shade to complete the look.

WEAR IT WELL...

Follow these simple steps to be the best-dressed girl on the beach.

1 Make a splash with a snazzy swimsuit or bikini. Stripy and floral patterns are a great buy as they look super stylish and are forever fashionable.

2 Sandals are a fashion essential for this look. Flip-flops are a must have if you're hitting the beach, but open-toe and gladiator styles will make a style statement.

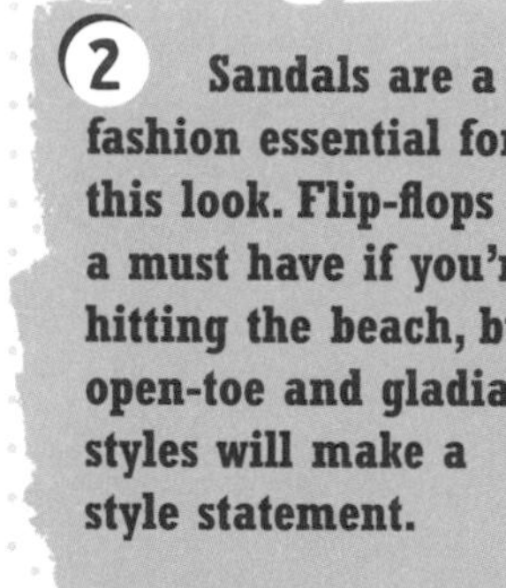

3 Stay cool in a long floaty maxi dress. They look great with a little layering, so add a denim jacket and belt and wear with flat shoes.

4 Keep it casual with cut-off faded denim shorts and a simple vest. Turn to page 109 to make your own shorts.

5 Cover-up with a pretty sundress in a bright colour. Wear it over your swimwear in the day and add some jewellery and sandals for a great day-to-night look.

6 No holiday wardrobe is complete without a sun hat. Go glam with a chic fedora or panama hat, or keep it casual with a sporty cap.

DID YOU KNOW?

Light and white-coloured clothes reflect the sunshine, so they will help you keep cool when it's hot.

SUNGLASSES

Choosing the right shades can be tricky. Use our guide to work out the best style to suit your face.

STYLE SECRET

A bright tote bag is best for holding all your beach bits and bobs. It's not just practical but glamorous, too.

FACE SHAPE

ROUND	OVAL	SQUARE	HEART-SHAPED

GLASSES

ROUND	OVAL	SQUARE	HEART-SHAPED

Wide, rectangular frames	Any shape looks good	Round or oval	Round or cat eyes

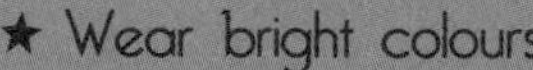

DO!

- ★ Wear bright colours.
- ★ Team tight shorts with a loose-fitting top.
- ★ Go retro with high-waisted bikini bottoms and oversized shades.
- ★ Wear a sunhat to protect your skin and hair.

DON'T!

- ★ Wear black all over. You'll bake!
- ★ Wear tight tops with tight shorts.
- ★ Opt for high heels. Flats are best.
- ★ Get sunburnt. Ouch!

Make it!

TRANSFORM YOUR SHOES!

Bored with your shoes? Grab a pair of plain, inexpensive ballet pumps and give them a makeover.

1 TOOLS: studs or sequins, glue
TIME: 10 mins plus drying time **SKILL LEVEL:** ✂

Stick on some sequins or studs to make your shoes sparkle. You can stick them all over or just in one area of the shoe, like the toe or heel.

Tip: instead of studs or sequins, stick some of your stickers onto your shoes instead.

2 TOOLS: tape measure, ribbon approx. 20 cm, scissors, glue, two buttons **TIME:** 15 mins **SKILL LEVEL:** ✂✂

★ Slip on your pump and measure the distance across the top of your foot, from one edge of the inside of the shoe to the other.

★ Add 3 cm to the measured length and cut a length of ribbon to this size. Glue one end of the ribbon to the inside of the shoe.

★ Stick the other end of the ribbon to the outside of the shoe on the opposite side. Glue a pretty button over this end of the ribbon. Repeat the whole process with the other shoe.

Tip: You can use card buttons to cover the ribbon ends instead of shop-bought ones.

3 TOOLS: newspaper, glue, glitter
TIME: 10 mins plus drying time **SKILL LEVEL:** ✂✂

Stuff your shoes with newspaper, then cover the shoes with glue. Shake red glitter all over, leave to dry and remove the newspaper for sparkling ruby slippers.

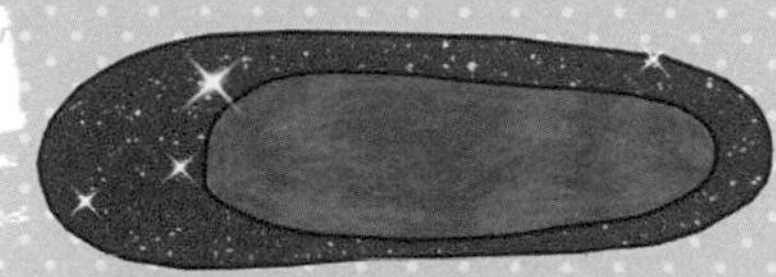

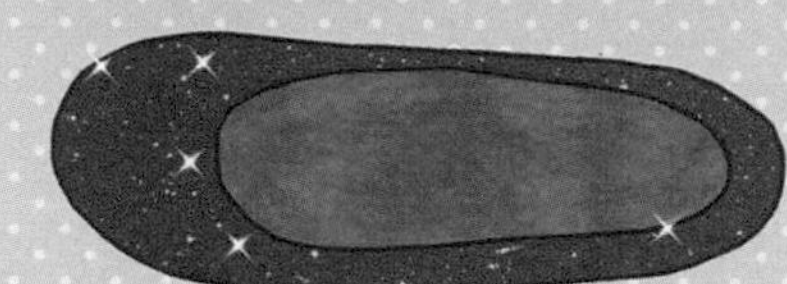

4 TOOLS: fabric pens **TIME:** 10 mins
SKILL LEVEL: ✂✂

Doodle some designs on your shoes. If you're not that good at drawing, just repeat an easy pattern over and over. Copy the one shown here or make up one of your own.

DO!
Ask a grown-up to help you with the coloured dye.

5 TOOLS: coloured dye, sponge
TIME: 10 mins plus drying time **SKILL LEVEL:** ✂✂✂

Choose a similar coloured dye to the colour of your shoe and prepare it in a pot. Carefully sponge some of the dye onto the toe area of your shoe and leave to dry. Repeat for the second shoe.

DID YOU KNOW?
The ballet pump is based on the ballet shoe, which was first worn by ballet dancers in the 16th century. Back then, ballet shoes had heels!

6 TOOLS: lace approx. 50 cm, scissors, glue **TIME:** 10 mins
SKILL LEVEL: ✂

Cut a length of lace trim and glue it around the top edge of your shoes for a delicate look. You could use a colour similar to that of your shoe or go for something completely different for a stylish contrast.

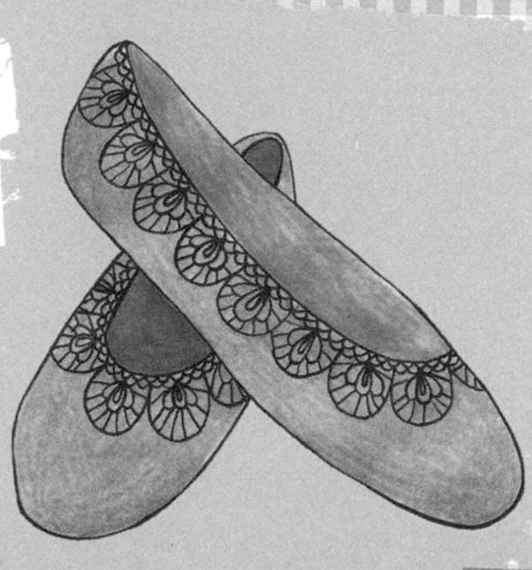

MONTH..

Stick, draw or stencil a picture of your BEST outfit here

FASHION FORECAST

Plan your outfits for the month here...

WHAT'S ON...	WHAT TO WEAR...
Parties & birthdays:	
....	....
....	....
Days out & holidays:	....
....	....
....	....
Other events:	....
....	....
....	....

Don't forget your SHOES!

Describe your BEST look of the month here

MY LOOK IS... ....

....

THE BEST BIT IS... ....

....

I WORE IT/WILL WEAR IT... ....

....

I BOUGHT IT/WILL BUY IT FROM... ....

....

THIS OUTFIT IS PERFECT FOR... HANGING OUT  **PARTIES** 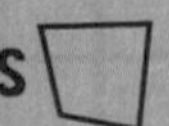 **SHOPPING** ☐

Design a hat to top off your outfit.

Draw some gloves to go with your look.

Don't forget the finishing touches to give your look the real wow factor!

What kind of necklace would you wear with this outfit and why?

....

....

Draw some stylish hair accessories here.

RATE YOUR LOOK

Give your outfit a score

/10

My friends

my look

DID YOU KNOW?

French designer Coco Chanel changed the way women dressed in the early 20th century. She created loose and comfortable clothing, which freed them from the old-fashioned corsets and fussy and frilly styles of the time.

GET THE LOOK

Whose look do you like this month? Stick or draw their pictures here.

STYLE SECRET

Before you buy an item, try to picture at least three places you can wear it. This way you won't buy clothes you end up never wearing.

STEAL THE STYLE

WINTER

Look cute and cosy all season long with our guide to the coolest winter wardrobe.

WEAR IT WELL...

Just because it's cold outside doesn't mean your clothes have to be boring and bulky.

1 Skinny jeans are a winter must have. They look great tucked into boots, and a vibrant-coloured pair will brighten up a dull day.

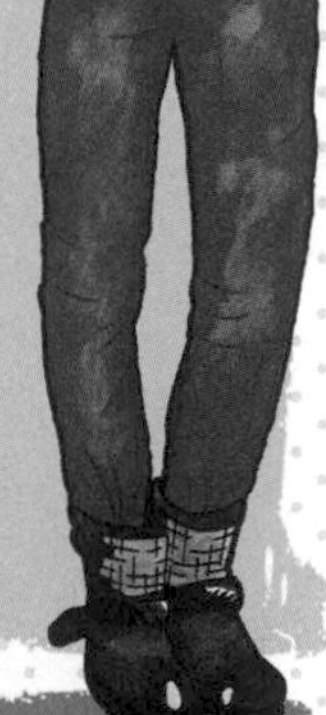

2 Pick a warm woolly hat that will go with your coat, skin and hair colour. Black and grey look best with blonde hair and if you have dark hair, try a lighter shade of wool.

3 Keep out the cold and stay on trend by adding layers. Wear a jacket and scarf over a jumper and layer your jumper over a shirt or longer t-shirt.

4 A scarf is one of the most useful and visible items of your winter ward-robe. A neutral colour will go with everything but a bright print or colour will add contrast to your look.

5 A long and slouchy boyfriend cardigan looks great buttoned up over leggings. For an alternative boho look wear open with a flowery dress.

6 Black or brown boots go with everything and look great with denim. To change the look, wear long coloured socks that show over the top of your boots.

FURRY FASHION

Wrap up in faux fur for an ultra-glam luxe look. A cosy coat is one way to wear this style but for a more subtle approach choose faux fur-edged gloves, hats and boots.

WINTER WARMER

Wool is not only cosy and comfy to wear it looks great too. The key to wearing it right is all about balance. Cable-knit jumpers and scarfs are very on-trend but can be chunky, so wear with skinny jeans, a pencil skirt or leggings to avoid looking too bulky.

COAT STYLES

These coats look oh so hot when it's oh so brrrrr outside...

STYLE SECRET

Combine bold clashing colours like blue and orange for a quirky and warm result.

MILITARY

Defined by its smart collar and shiny buttons, a military style coat will smarten up any outfit.

DUFFLE

The toggle fastenings and big patch pockets make this a cute option, and the large hood is very handy for keeping warm.

TRENCH

This stylish classic is best in black or beige. Button up and tighten that belt for a smart polished look.

PARKA

A true all-rounder, this coat will look great over everything. Avoid the over-shiny variety and opt for a faux fur collar and hood for extra style.

SEASONAL STYLE

A lack of sun doesn't mean you have to stop wearing your summer dresses. Follow these easy recycling tips for three fun and fresh looks.

1 Layer over leggings and a long-sleeved top.

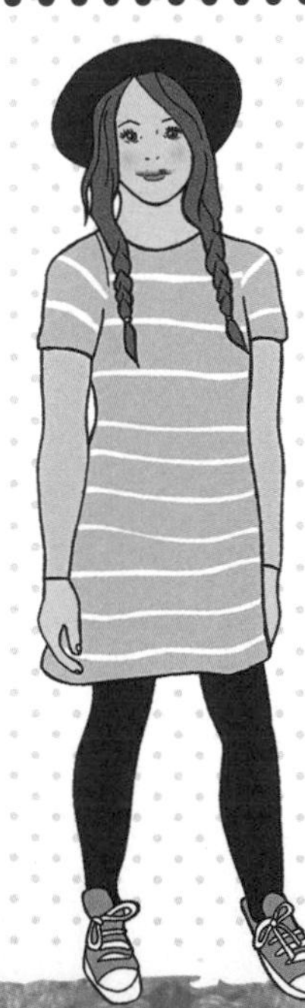

2 Wear with tights and a jumper over the top to turn your dress into a skirt.

3 Add a beanie, denim jacket, a scarf, long socks and boots for a girly grunge look.

LOOK OF THE MONTH

MONTH...

Stick, draw or stencil a picture of your BEST outfit here

FASHION FORECAST

Plan your outfits for the month here...

WHAT'S ON...

Parties & birthdays:

....

....

Days out & holidays:

....

....

Other events:

....

....

WHAT TO WEAR...

....

....

....

....

....

....

....

....

Don't forget your SHOES!

Describe your BEST look of the month here

MY LOOK IS... ....

....

THE BEST BIT IS... ....

....

I WORE IT/WILL WEAR IT... ....

....

I BOUGHT IT/WILL BUY IT FROM... ....

....

THIS OUTFIT IS PERFECT FOR... **HANGING OUT** ☐ **PARTIES** ☐  **SHOPPING** ☐

Create some shoes to go with your look
Design a brooch to finish off your outfit.
Don't forget the finishing touches to give your look the real wow factor!
What perfume would suit your look?
What colour bag would look good with your outfit?
RATE YOUR LOOK
Give your outfit a score
/10
My friends
my look
DID YOU KNOW?
The first lady's boot was designed for Queen Victoria of Great Britain in 1840.
GET THE LOOK
Whose look do you like this month? Stick or draw their pictures here.
My fave celebrity look
Best look on a friend
STYLE SECRET
Don't keep squeezing more clothes into your wardrobe. If you haven't worn anything for a year, give it to a friend or a charity shop.

STEAL THE STYLE

FESTIVAL CHIC

You don't have to go to a festival to rock this stylish look – it's great for everyday wear too.

WEAR IT WELL...

Check out these festival chic essentials and the best ways to wear them.

1 The key item for your look is a pair of denim shorts. Faded and frayed at the edges is the classic way to wear them, but high-waisted ones are a smart alternative.

2 Number two on your shopping list is a cool pair of wellies. Go for a crazy design if you want to stand out from the crowd.

3 Embrace your inner rock chick with a t-shirt with a bold motif or slogan. Check out some great ways to customize your own t-shirt on page 82.

4 Denim or leather jackets always look stylish, but for a more boho look try a suede or fringed waistcoat.

5 Festival chic should look effortless so mix different accessories together, like bead and metal bracelets, for a glam but casual appearance.

6 Top your look off with a cute fedora hat.

MAKE YOUR MARK

Add a touch of glamour to your festival look with some manicure magic. Two-tone nails, a dotty nail pattern or sparkly glittered nails all look great but if your nail-painting skills aren't up to it, cheat with some cool nail art stickers instead.

DO!

Swap the wellies for sandals or trainers if the sun is shining.

DON'T!

Forget your shades. Wayfarers or aviator styles are best for serious festival fashionistas.

WHATS YOUR STYLE?

Check out the shopping lists below and tick which items you'd buy to reveal your festival style.

A

- denim jacket ☐
- stripy vest ☐
- shorts ☐
- aviator sunglasses ☐
- wellies ☐

B

- leather jacket ☐
- black t-shirt ☐
- jeans ☐
- wayfarer sunglasses ☐
- biker boots ☐

C

- waistcoat ☐
- floral blouse ☐
- floaty skirt ☐
- mirrored sunglasses ☐
- sandals ☐

MOSTLY As
on-trend festival wear

MOSTLY Bs
rock 'n' roll

MOSTLY Cs
boho flower power

FESTIVAL HAIR

Try out these quick and easy hairstyles...

1 Make a daisy-chain garland by sewing or sticking daisy flowers to a piece of black elastic.

2 If you are having a bad hair day just cover up with a bright bandana.

3 Pretty plaits always look great. They're easy to do and can be left in overnight to create a wavy style for the next day.

DIY FESTIVAL FABULOUS

Customizing your old clothes is a great way to create your own unique festival wardrobe, without having to spend a penny. Try adding some stick-on jewels or studs to your denim shorts or cut strips along the bottom of an old vest to make a cool fringed top.

Make it!

TRANSFORM A PAIR OF JEANS

Take one pair of jeans and add a bit of DIY chic for five stylish makeovers.

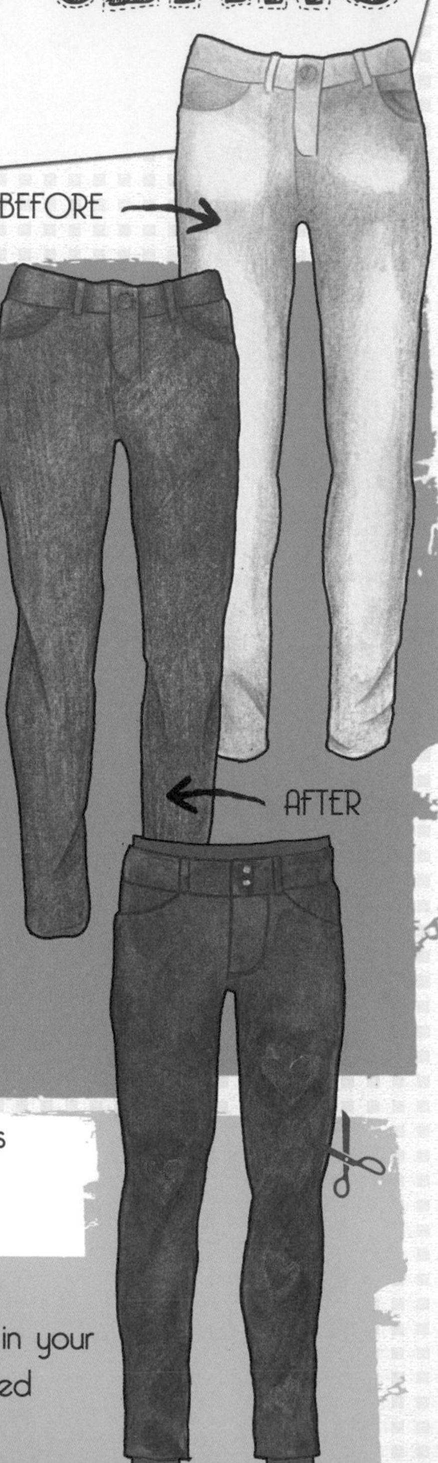

1 TOOLS: jeans, bucket, rubber gloves, wooden spoon, fabric dye **TIME:** 45 mins plus washing and drying time **SKILL LEVEL:** ✂✂

Love your jeans but not their colour? No problem, just dye them.

★ Fill your bucket with hot water and dye (according to the instructions on the dye box). Run your jeans under hot water, then put on your rubber gloves and put them in the bucket of dye. Stir them with a wooden spoon for around 10 minutes for a light dye job and up to 30 minutes for a darker one.

★ Take out your jeans and rinse with water until the water runs clean then wash them in the washing machine, leaving them to air dry.

Tip: use your stencil skills to help create peep holes with different shapes.

2 TOOLS: jeans, scissors, leggings or tights **TIME:** 20 mins **SKILL LEVEL:** ✂✂

Create some cute no-sew patches.

★ Cut some heart-shaped holes in your jeans and wear them with coloured tights or leggings underneath.

3 **TOOLS:** old jeans, scissors, needle, thread, ribbon (1.5 m), measuring tape, fabric pens, accessories to decorate
TIME: 10 mins
SKILL LEVEL: ✂✂

Create a nifty holder for your phone or MP3 player.

★ Cut around the seams of the back pocket of your old jeans.

★ Measure and cut a length of ribbon that will reach from the front of your waist, over your shoulder to the back of your waist. With a couple of stitches, attach the ends of the ribbon to both sides of the back of the pocket to create a cross-body strap for your holder.

★ Decorate with accessories or stickers.

4 **TOOLS:** jeans, 3 paintbrushes, 3 fabric paint colours, newspaper
TIME: 30 mins plus drying time
SKILL LEVEL: ✂✂

Paint-splattered jeans are a big trend on the catwalk, so try this!

★ Lay an old pair of jeans on sheets of newspaper on the floor.

★ Using a paintbrush, brush some random strokes on your jeans. Then take another paintbrush and paint some more strokes and splats in a different colour.

★ For the finishing touch, take a third paintbrush with a final colour and gently flick or dab spots of paint on your jeans. Leave to dry overnight.

5 **TOOLS:** jeans, scissors, measuring tape, chalk, ruler **TIME:** 20 mins
SKILL LEVEL: ✂✂

Transform your jeans into a pair of shorts.

★ Measure about 30 cm down from the waistband on one leg and mark with some chalk. Using this mark and a ruler, draw a straight line across the jean leg.

★ Cut along the line then cut the second leg to match the length of the first.

★ Roll up each leg two or three times to the desired length.

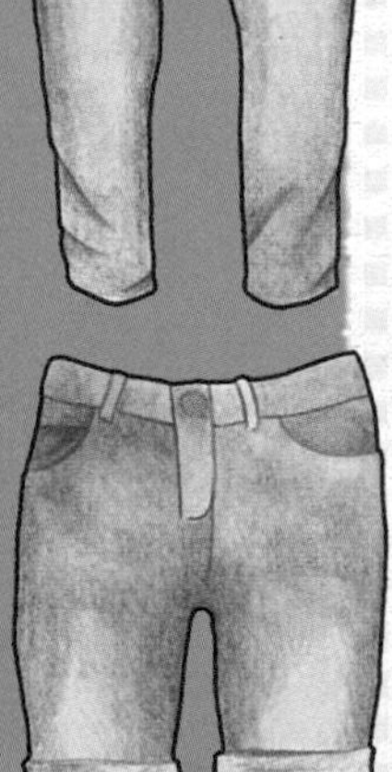

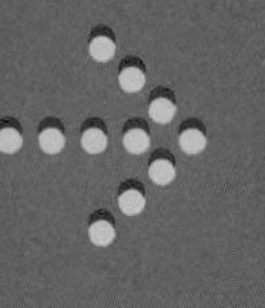

LOOK OF THE MONTH

MONTH...

Stick, draw or stencil a picture of your BEST outfit here

FASHION FORECAST

Plan your outfits for the month here...

WHAT'S ON...

Parties & birthdays:

....

....

Days out & holidays:

....

....

Other events:

....

....

WHAT TO WEAR...

....

....

....

....

....

....

....

Don't forget your SHOES!

Describe your BEST look of the month here

MY LOOK IS... ....

....

THE BEST BIT IS... ....

....

I WORE IT/WILL WEAR IT... ....

....

I BOUGHT IT/WILL BUY IT FROM... ....

....

THIS OUTFIT IS PERFECT FOR... HANGING OUT 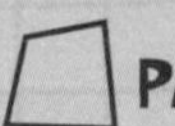 **PARTIES** ☐ **SHOPPING** 

Design some accessories to go with your outfit.

What kind of bracelet would suit your look? Design it here.

Don't forget the finishing touches to give your look the real wow factor!

What shape sunglasses would you choose for your look? ....

Would straight, curly or tied up hair suit your look best? Draw a style here.

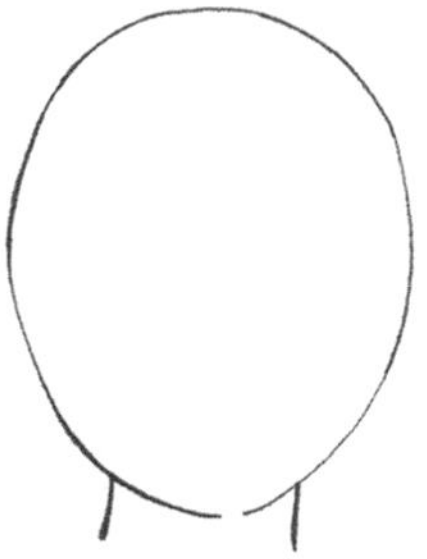

RATE YOUR LOOK

Give your outfit a score

/10

My friends

my look

DID YOU KNOW?

There are about 40 Fashion Weeks in different cities throughout the year, but the biggest are held in New York, Milan, Paris and London.

GET THE LOOK

Whose look do you like this month? Stick or draw their pictures here.

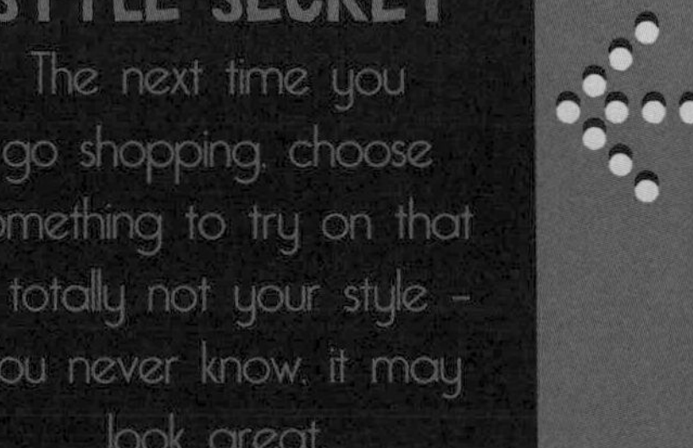

STYLE SECRET

The next time you go shopping, choose something to try on that is totally not your style – you never know, it may look great.

PARTY TIME

Planning your party look? Dress to impress with these great styles.

WEAR IT WELL...

For a party-perfect look every time, follow these simple rules.

1 If you want to wear jeans, dress them up with a sparkly top and jewellery.

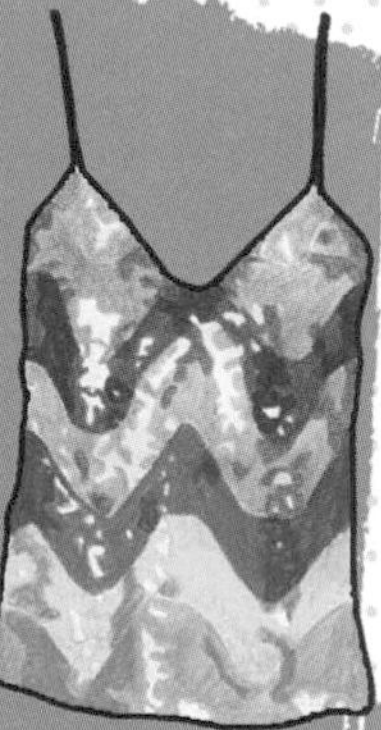

2 Avoid the fashion faux-pas of wearing the same outfit as someone else by making your look unique. You could alter the length of your prom dress or wear it with a denim jacket and biker boots.

3 A party is a great time to experiment with your make-up. Pick one feature to highlight and try something new. Bright blue or green eyeshadow will define the eyes. Or create the perfect pout with a bold pink or red lipstick.

4 A party is the perfect time to wear heels, but if you get a a bit wobbly in high heels opt for cute kitten heels or wedges instead.

5 The little black dress is a party staple, but printed midis and floaty maxis are another option if you don't want to play it safe with a classic.

6 Make an effort to do something different with your hair. If it's long, slick it down with serum into a glamorous side parting. For short hair, add a sparkly headband.

PARTY GLITTER

Add some sparkle to your look with dramatic earrings, some serious arm-candy bracelets, cocktail rings and a collar necklace. See page 88 for how to make your own. Don't be afraid to pile on the bling – when it comes to a party, it's your time to shine.

STYLE SECRET

Not sure if you want to wear a long or short dress to your party? For the best of both worlds, rock a high-low dress instead (short at the front, long at the back).

WHAT KIND OF PARTY GIRL ARE YOU?

1 At a party you like to...

A dance ☐

B check out everyone else's outfits ☐

C chat to your friends ☐

2 The accessory you can't live without is...

A your phone ☐

B your brand-new handbag ☐

C your pearl earrings ☐

3 Your party preparation time is at least...

A half an hour ☐

B a week before ☐

C one to two hours ☐

4 Your favourite style of dress is...

A one you can move in ☐

B the latest style ☐

C a sweet prom dress ☐

5 Your shoe of choice is...

A something comfy ☐

B sparkly heels ☐

C pretty and pink ☐

MOSTLY As

Disco Diva – opt for a bright, lycra dress over cool leggings and flat pumps.

MOSTLY Bs

Style Queen – choose cropped trousers with a peplum top and heels.

MOSTLY Cs

Party Princess – try a pink tulip dress with heels.

TOP THAT!

Sticking to the tried-and-tested party formula of a stylish top and jeans needn't be predictable when there are so many different styles of top to choose from.

1 A favourite choice with fashionistas, the peplum top will add definition to your waist and a smart edge to your outfit.

2 The crop top is very on-trend but if you don't want to expose too much of your midriff, wear with high-waisted jeans.

3 An attractive bandeau or strapless top creates a dramatic neckline to show off your best jewellery.

Make it!

A BELT

It may be a small accessory, but a belt can have a big impact on an outfit. Check out these quick and easy ways to create and wear one.

1 TOOLS: a scarf
TIME: 2 mins **SKILL LEVEL:** ✂

Wrap a twisted scarf around your waist and knot at the side for a simple way to accessorize a plain dress.

2 TOOLS: tape measure, scissors, tyre, paper fasteners
TIME: 15 mins
SKILL LEVEL: ✂✂

Next time your bike gets a puncture, save the tyre and cut it up to create an edgy rubber belt.

★ Give the tyre a good wash to remove any dirt.

★ Measure around your waist and cut the tyre to the size required, trimming the edges to get the width you want as well as the length.

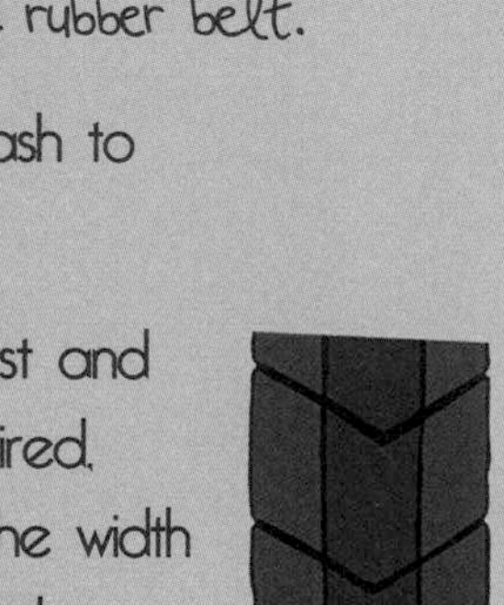

★ Wrap the tyre belt around your waist and mark where you want it to fasten at each end.

★ Using a pair of sharp scissors, poke a hole in each end of the belt, line up the holes and poke a paper fastener through the holes to secure the belt around your waist. You could add more paper fasteners along the belt to create a studded effect.

3 TOOLS: tape measure, scissors, thin rope about 2 metres, safety pin
TIME: 15 mins **SKILL LEVEL:** ✂✂

Transform some rope into a cool nautical-style belt.

★ Measure around your waist, add an extra 30 cm and cut three strips of thin rope to this length.

★ Leave 15 cm and tie the lengths of rope together in a small knot. Pin the ropes to a stationary object, like a cushion, and plait the ropes until you're 15 cm from the end. Then tie another knot.

★ Loop around your waist and knot at the front.

4 **TOOLS:** tape measure, scissors, tie, popper fastener, needle, thread **TIME:** 20 minutes **SKILL LEVEL:** ✂✂✂

Ask your dad if you can have one of his old ties to make a cool belt.

★ Choose a bright and bold-patterned tie and lay it on a flat surface. Measure around your waist and add an extra 10 cm and cut the tie to this length. Make sure you cut the fatter end of the tie, so your belt will be a more even width.

★ Fold over the edges of the end you have cut into a point and sew a neat line of stitches along the edges, to tidy it up. Sew one half of the popper fastener to the reverse of the pointed end, and the other half to the correct side of the other end so the belt fits you.

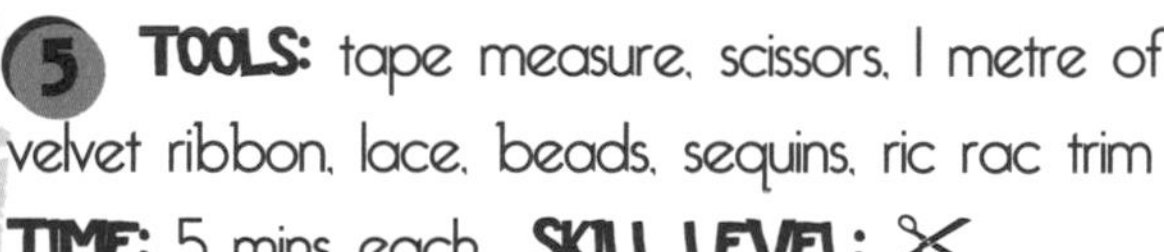

5 **TOOLS:** tape measure, scissors, 1 metre of velvet ribbon, lace, beads, sequins, ric rac trim **TIME:** 5 mins each **SKILL LEVEL:** ✂

Add a bit of luxe to your jeans with a thick velvet ribbon belt.

★ Measure around your waist, add an extra 30 cm and cut a length of ribbon to size. Loop through your jeans' waistband and tie at the front in a stylish bow.

★ For more belts in this style, follow the instructions above to create belts in:

Belt Up

Get the best out of your belt with these simple rules...

1 Try out your belt above, below and on your waistline to find the best position.

2 Pick a belt that contrasts with your outfit, to draw attention to your waist.

3 Where possible, choose a belt that has some elastic in because it'll stretch with you, making it more comfortable to wear.

4 Wrap a belt over a cardigan, jumper or jacket for an instant style update.

LOOK OF THE MONTH

MONTH..

Stick, draw or stencil a picture of your BEST outfit here

FASHION FORECAST

Plan your outfits for the month here...

WHAT'S ON...	WHAT TO WEAR...
Parties & birthdays:	
....	....
....	....
Days out & holidays:	....
....	....
....	....
Other events:	....
....	....
....	....

Don't forget your SHOES!

Describe your BEST look of the month here

MY LOOK IS... ....

....

THE BEST BIT IS... ....

....

I WORE IT/WILL WEAR IT... ....

....

I BOUGHT IT/WILL BUY IT FROM... ....

....

THIS OUTFIT IS PERFECT FOR... HANGING OUT ☐ PARTIES ☐ SHOPPING ☐

Design a shoulder bag to go with your outfit.

Draw a cool ring to finish off your look.

Don't forget the finishing touches to give your look the real wow factor!

What kind of hat would suit your look?

....

Doodle some cool designs for your nails.

RATE YOUR LOOK

Give your outfit a score

/10

My friends

my look

DID YOU KNOW?

The discovery of Tutankhamun's tomb in Egypt in the 1920s led to Egyptian-style art on handbags and purses.

GET THE LOOK

Whose look do you like this month? Stick or draw their pictures here.

STYLE SECRET

For an instant and up-to-date fashion fix, snip a slit to create a split ankle in an old pair of jeans or trousers.

NAUTICAL STYLE

Look to the high seas for an inspired look that will never go out of fashion.

WEAR IT WELL...

For effortless nautical style, follow these simple rules...

1 Sailor stripes look great with everything. Go super smart with a stripy blazer or keep it casual with a stripy vest.

2 Create an instant nautical look with symbols like an anchor or rope on your clothes and accessories.

3 For a bit of bling, pick jackets and jumpers with shiny buttons.

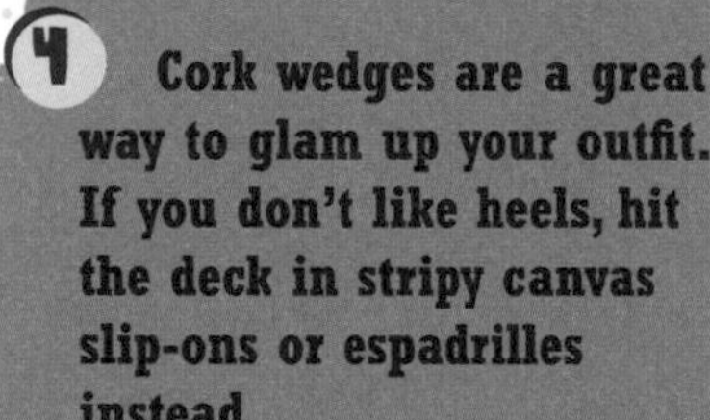

4 Cork wedges are a great way to glam up your outfit. If you don't like heels, hit the deck in stripy canvas slip-ons or espadrilles instead.

5 For bags of nautical style, sling a canvas bag with leather or rope handles over your shoulder.

DIVE IN

Get the look with a fun and fresh nautical swimming costume or bikini. You can't go wrong with classic stripes, but gold edging and rope fastenings look great, too. For an instant update to an old plain swimsuit, use some stencils to draw an anchor or starfish symbol on the front with fabric pens or paint.

DID YOU KNOW?

The navy-and-white-striped top dates back to 1858, when it became part of the French Navy's uniform, as it made it easier to spot sailors who fell overboard.

SAILOR CHIC

If you only have one sea-inspired item in your wardrobe, make it a stripy top. It's very versatile and can be worn in lots of ways.

COLOUR CODE

The most important nautical colours are red, white and blue. Use them to design a stripy pattern on this vest.

STYLE SECRET

The secret to sailor chic is to keep it simple. Don't go overboard with too many stripes.

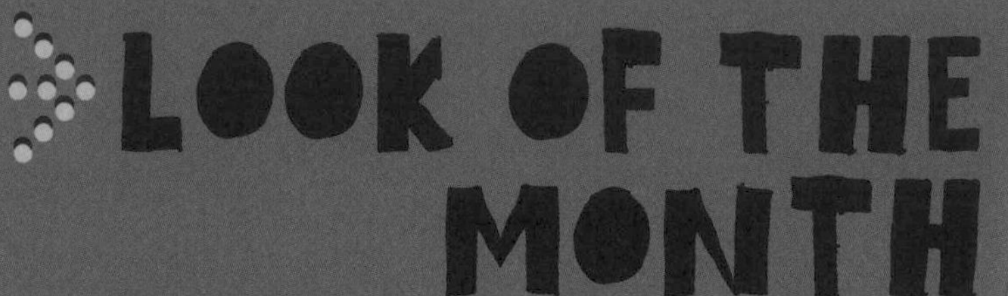

LOOK OF THE MONTH

MONTH..

Stick, draw or stencil a picture of your BEST outfit here

FASHION FORECAST

Plan your outfits for the month here...

WHAT'S ON...

Parties & birthdays:

....

....

Days out & holidays:

....

....

Other events:

....

....

WHAT TO WEAR...

....

....

....

....

....

....

....

....

Don't forget your SHOES!

Describe your BEST look of the month here

MY LOOK IS... ....

....

THE BEST BIT IS... ....

....

I WORE IT/WILL WEAR IT... ....

....

I BOUGHT IT/WILL BUY IT FROM... ....

....

THIS OUTFIT IS PERFECT FOR... HANGING OUT ☐ **PARTIES**  **SHOPPING** ☐

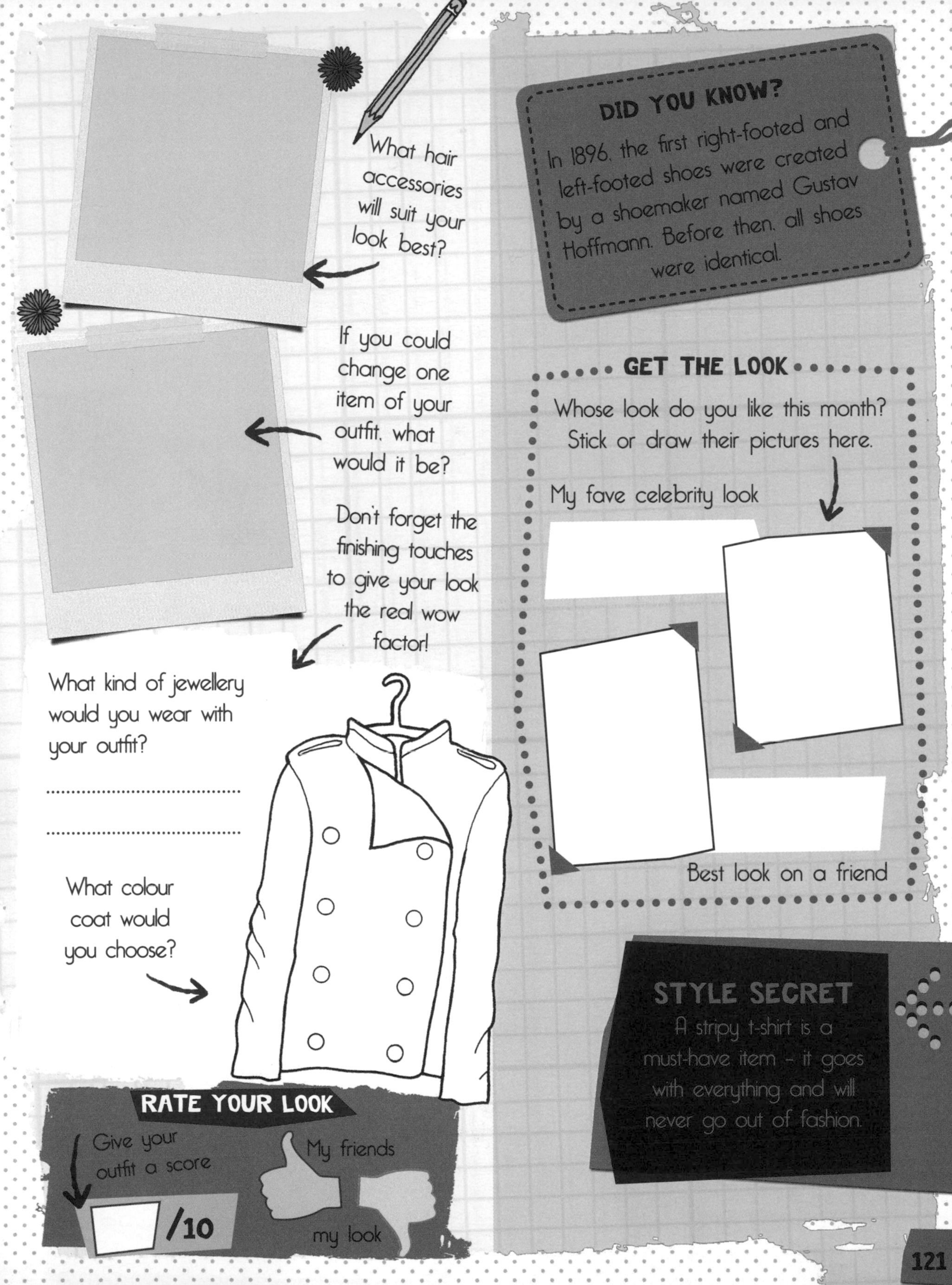
What hair accessories will suit your look best?
If you could change one item of your outfit, what would it be?
Don't forget the finishing touches to give your look the real wow factor!
What kind of jewellery would you wear with your outfit?
What colour coat would you choose?
RATE YOUR LOOK
Give your outfit a score
/10
My friends
my look
DID YOU KNOW?
In 1896, the first right-footed and left-footed shoes were created by a shoemaker named Gustav Hoffmann. Before then, all shoes were identical.
GET THE LOOK
Whose look do you like this month? Stick or draw their pictures here.
My fave celebrity look
Best look on a friend
STYLE SECRET
A stripy t-shirt is a must-have item – it goes with everything and will never go out of fashion.

STEAL THE STYLE

ROCK CHICK

This look has it all – it's grungy, edgy, feminine and it totally rocks.

BIKER BABE STYLE

The biker look is similar to the rock chick style but needs a lot more leather to pull it off. Get the look with a studded belt, boots and a knotted scarf around your neck.

WEAR IT WELL...

Try these top tips to rock this look.

1 Avoid wearing bright colours – black is best. If you want to wear any other colours, stick with white, grey and red.

2 You can never have too much denim. Black jeans are a must-have but grey, stonewashed and blue denim look good too.

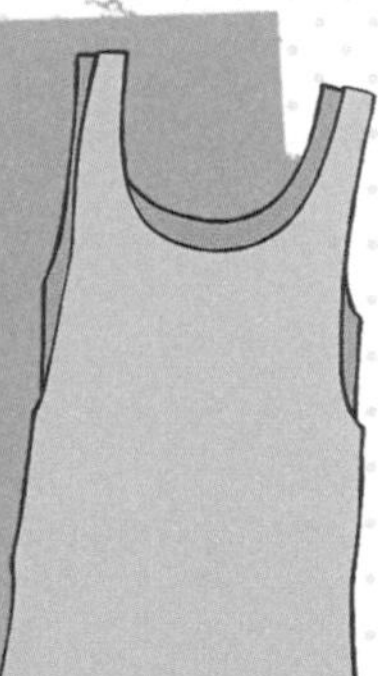

3 For a casual look, layer long vests in greys and blacks over each other.

4 All true rock chicks have at least one cool t-shirt in their wardrobe. Go for one with a band name or a skull and crossbones on.

5 Go grungy and gutsy with your hairstyle. Spike short hair up for a punk vibe or use curling irons or hair straightners to create unruly waves if you have longer hair.

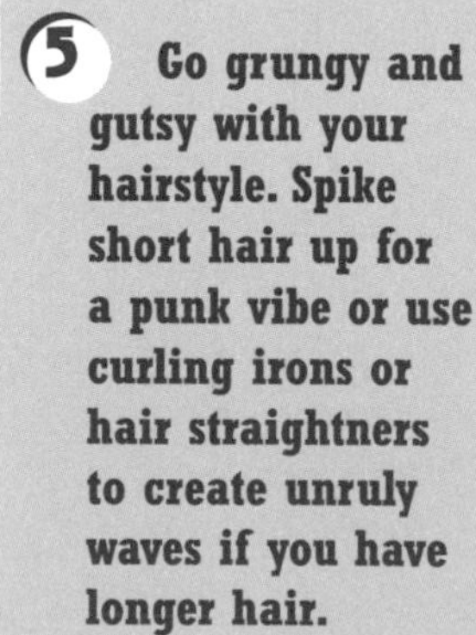

6 Biker boots and pump trainers are the casual and comfy footwear option but slip into a pair of studded heels to inject some hard-core glamour.

STYLE SECRET

Don't care about what anyone else thinks. Being a rock chick is all about doing your own thing and breaking all the fashion rules.

GET THE LOOK

If you only have one rock-chick item in your wardrobe, make it a black leather (or leather-look) jacket. This classic piece never goes out of fashion.

FINISHING TOUCHES

Add attitude to your outfit with some black wayfarer sunglasses, a scarf with an edgy skull pattern and stacks of jewellery. Wear chunky chains and large hoop earrings together and choose a bracelet with quirky charms, like hearts, feathers, music notes and crosses.

Add some charms to this bracelet to create your own rock chic design.

DO!

If you like wearing make-up, volumize your eyelashes with multiple coats of mascara and line your eyelids with black eyeliner.

DON'T!

Wear this look when it's really sunny - black attracts the sunlight and will leave you feeling hot rather than looking it.

Make it! JEWELLERY

Add the perfect finishing touch to your look with these unique and homemade jewellery designs.

1 TOOLS: hoop earrings, 2 buttons
TIME: 2 mins
SKILL LEVEL: ✂

Thread buttons onto an existing pair of small hoop earrings to create a nifty new pair in an instant.

2 TOOLS: approx. 85 safety pins, coloured beads, measuring tape, thin elastic about 20 cm, scissors
TIME: 40 mins **SKILL LEVEL:** ✂✂✂

Recycle safety pins and create a cool bead bracelet.

★ Take a safety pin, fill the pin with coloured beads and close it. Repeat this step for 85 pins.

★ Cut two lengths of elastic, measuring 10 cm, to thread the pins together. To start, tie a knot at one end of each of the elastics and thread one length of elastic through the head of a safety pin. Then, thread the second length of elastic through the circle hole at the bottom of that safety pin.

★ Continue adding safety pins in this way. When the last pin is added, tie the ends.

3 TOOLS: stretchy beading cord, tape measure, needle, beads, scissors.
TIME: 5 mins per ring **SKILL LEVEL:** ✂

These sweet rings are so quick and easy to make, you'll be able to make lots to stack on your finger.

★ Cut some stretchy beading cord about 15 cm long and thread it through a needle. Thread on different colour beads to cover approx. 5 cm.

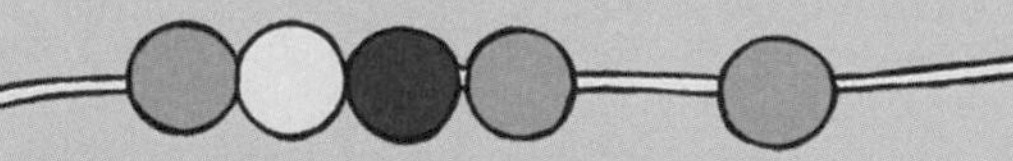

★ Tie a knot in the cord, to join up the beads and snip off the excess cord.

★ Roll onto your finger and start the next one.

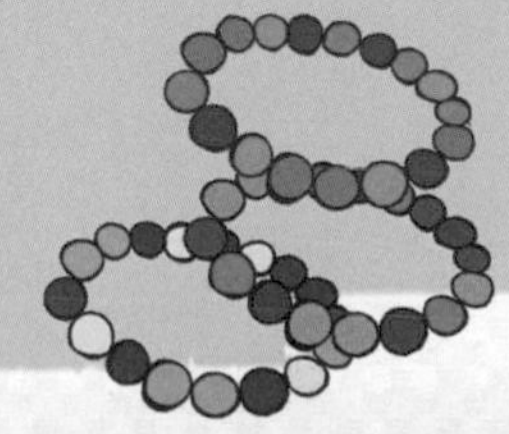

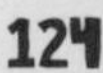

4

TOOLS: black thin ribbon 1.5 metres, scissors, tape measure, about 20 hex nuts, safety pin **TIME:** 20 mins **SKILL LEVEL:** ✂✂

This clever make creates a stylish and edgy necklace using just ribbon and nuts.

★ Cut your ribbon into three 50 cm strands and tie them together in a small knot. Pin them to a stationary object, like a cushion, using a safety pin and plait the three strands for about 15 cm. Before you plait the next strand add a hex nut and then proceed to plait it over the strand in the middle as normal.

★ Proceed to do this for each strand for a further 20 cm, then plait the last 15 cm without adding any nuts and when you come to the end tie the strands together in a small knot. Fasten the necklace around your neck by tying the plaited strand ends in a knot or bow.

5

TOOLS: ice-lolly sticks, pan of water and a hob to boil it on, jam jar, paints, fabric pens, glitter, wool, glue to decorate **TIME:** 60 mins plus overnight drying time **SKILL LEVEL:** ✂✂✂

Make cool cuff bracelets from ice-lolly sticks.

★ Collect old ice-lolly sticks or buy a bag from a craft shop or supermarket. Boil them in a pan of water for about 30 minutes. Boil more than you need as some won't be good enough to use.

★ Once they have softened, drain the sticks, then gently curve the sticks and place them in a jar or glass to hold their shape.

★ Allow the sticks to dry overnight, then they are ready to be decorated. You can paint them, stick on glitter or wrap wool around them for lots of different designs.

LOOK OF THE MONTH

MONTH..

Stick, draw or stencil a picture of your BEST outfit here

FASHION FORECAST

Plan your outfits for the month here...

WHAT'S ON...

Parties & birthdays:

....

....

Days out & holidays:

....

....

Other events:

....

....

WHAT TO WEAR...

....

....

....

....

....

....

....

....

Don't forget your SHOES!

Describe your BEST look of the month here

MY LOOK IS... ....

....

THE BEST BIT IS... ....

....

I WORE IT/WILL WEAR IT... ....

....

I BOUGHT IT/WILL BUY IT FROM... ....

....

THIS OUTFIT IS PERFECT FOR... HANGING OUT ☐ **PARTIES** ☐ **SHOPPING** ☐

Draw a stylish watch to go with your look.

What necklace would you wear with your outfit?

Don't forget the finishing touches to give your look the real wow factor!

What hairstyle would suit your style?

....

....

Add a splash of colour to your outfit with a bright wallet.

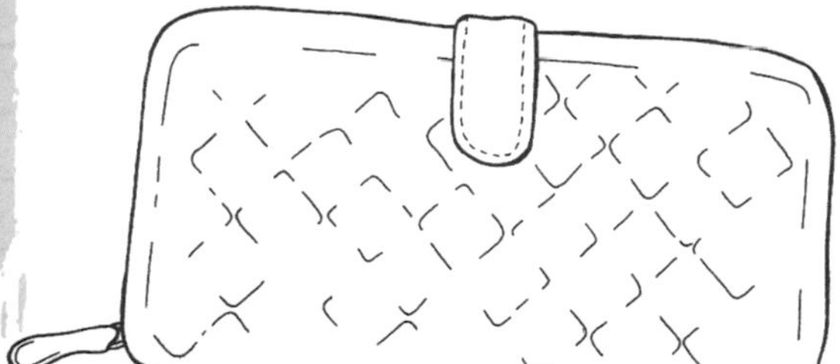

RATE YOUR LOOK

Give your outfit a score

/10

My friends my look

DID YOU KNOW?

Ancient Egyptians wore eye make-up to look good but also to protect their eyes from infection.

GET THE LOOK

Whose look do you like this month? Stick or draw their pictures here.

My fave celebrity look

Best look on a friend

STYLE SECRET

A bit of contrast makes a great style statement. Try a leather jacket over a prom dress or a stylish necklace over a plain t-shirt.

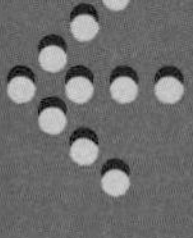

STEAL THE STYLE

BRIGHT & BOLD

Loud and proud colours are bang on trend. All you have to do is find the shade you'll shine in.

WEAR IT WELL...

Add a burst of colour to your outfit for an instant confidence boost.

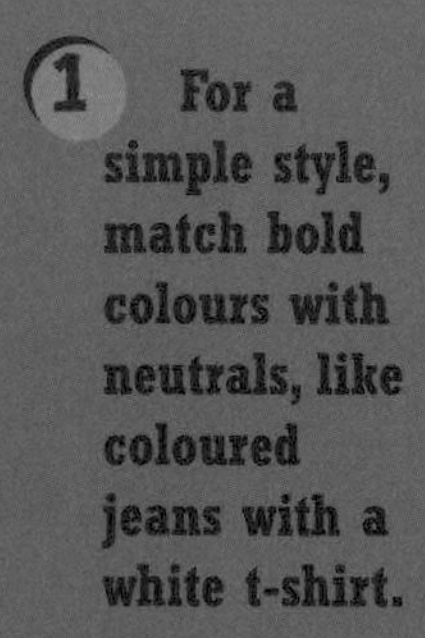

1 For a simple style, match bold colours with neutrals, like coloured jeans with a white t-shirt.

2 Choose complementary, or contrasting, colours for your top and bottom for an on-trend colour-block look.

3 Don't wear more than three colours at a time, otherwise your look will be more Coco the Clown than Coco Chanel.

4 Add a shot of neon to an already bright outfit for an even more dazzling effect.

5 When wearing brightly coloured accessories, go easy on your clothes and stick to neutrals.

6 Treat yourself to a make-up makeover and try a different-coloured eyeliner, eyeshadow or lipstick.

SHINY STYLE

Metallic bronze, silver and gold clothes are perfect for an effortless look as they don't need accessorizing with jewellery. For maximum impact team with a brightly coloured handbag or shoes.

NEON EXTRAS

If you're a fan of neon, look to use it in your accessories. A shocking-green handbag, bright orange scarf or neon yellow shoes will inject a fresh burst of colour and ensure your look is up-to-date.

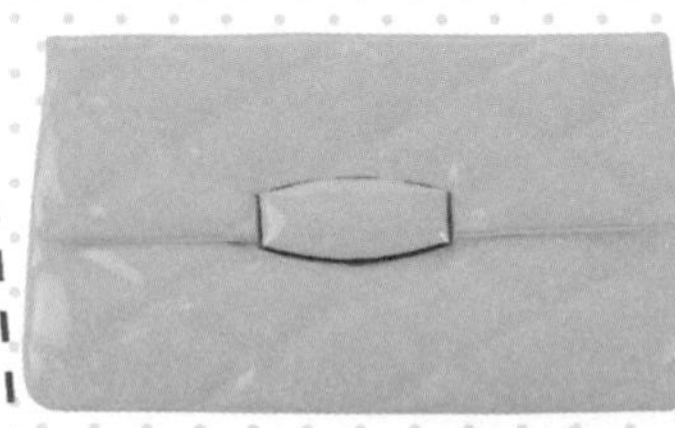

COLOUR WHEEL

The colour wheel is a useful fashion tool and will help you work out which colours to wear together.

★ Colours that sit directly next to each other, like yellow and yellow-orange.

★ Colours that form right angles with each other, like yellow and red-orange.

★ Colours directly opposite each other like yellow and violet.

★ Colours that form a T, like blue, orange and violet-red.

★ Colours that form an 'X', like blue, orange, violet-red and yellow.

★ White, black and brown are neutral and will go with anything.

Colour in these outfits to create some stylish colour combinations.

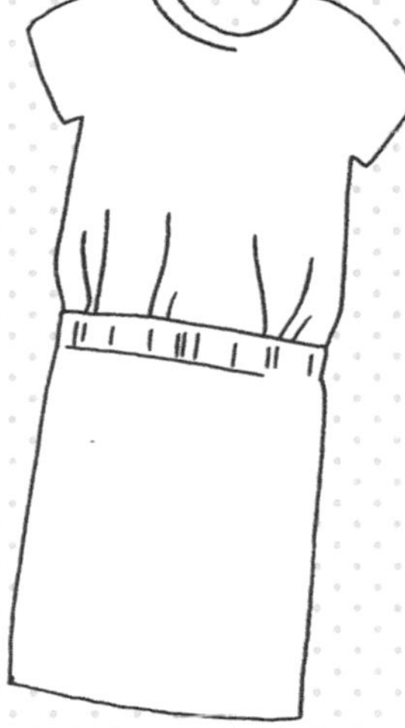

WHAT COLOURS SUIT YOU?

It's fun to experiment with colour and you should wear any colour you want to, but for a great look every time, find out what colours suit you best.

DARKER SKIN TONES tend to have warmer undertones like olives and gold, which suit colours like reds, oranges, yellows and dark browns.

FAIRER SKIN TONES tend to have more pink and cooler undertones and suit pink, blue, purple and green colours.

Make it!

HOW TO EMBROIDER

Customize your clothes with cute embroidery patches.

TOOLS: tracing paper, pencil, fabric swatch approx. 10 cm x 10 cm, needle, threads, scissors **TIME:** approx. 30 mins to 1 hour **SKILL LEVEL:** ✂✂

Make your own patches with one of these patterns, or design your own.

How to make your patch

★ Pick an embroidery pattern below and trace over it using a pencil and tracing paper.

★ Lay your tracing paper face down onto your fabric swatch and draw firmly over the shape to transfer the pencil marks onto the fabric.

★ Stitch over your pencil marks with your chosen coloured threads.

How to sew

Sewing and embroidery are useful skills for customizing clothes. If you don't know how, here are the basics.

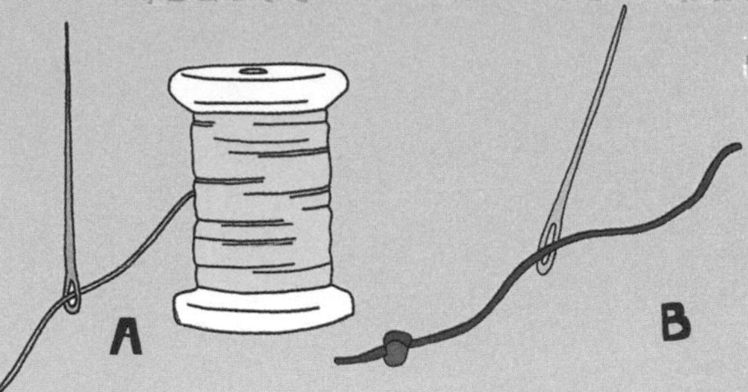

★ Pass a length of thread through the eye (hole) in your needle (A) and tie a knot at the end to secure (B).

SATIN STITCH

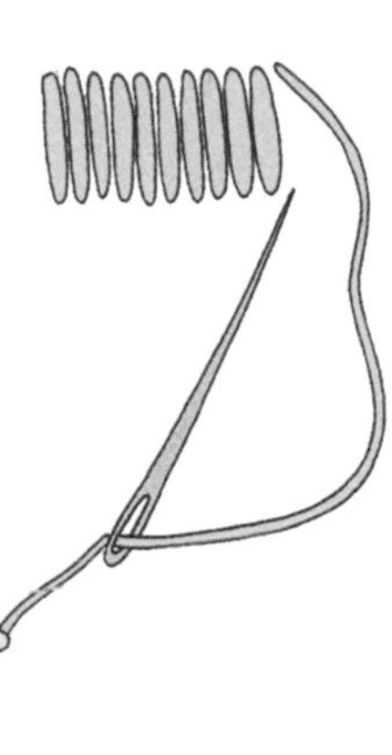

A satin stitch allows you to decorate a simple pattern.

★ Sew straight parallel stitches across the shape or pattern you are making.

RUNNING STITCH

A running stitch is the most straightforward embroidery stitch and easy to learn and use.

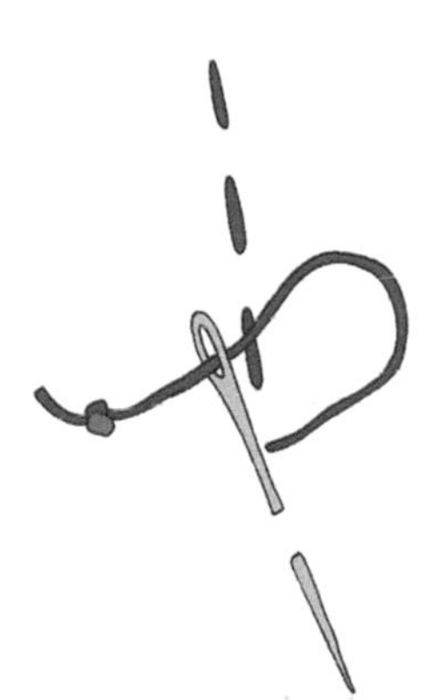

★ Push the needle back and forth through your fabric at equal points for a neat stitch that will hold your fabric together or create a pretty pattern.

Uniquely yours

You can use your embroidered patches to customize your clothes and accessories. Sew them on to re-invent old favourites from your jeans, t-shirts and gloves to a bag or pencil case.

DO!

For a more professional finish, stitch through two layers of fabric instead of one, so you can't see through the fabric to any knots and tangles at the back.

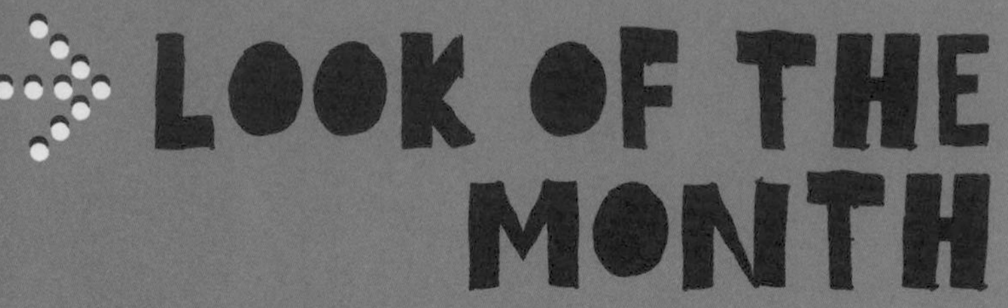

LOOK OF THE MONTH

MONTH..

Stick, draw or stencil a picture of your BEST outfit here

FASHION FORECAST

Plan your outfits for the month here...

WHAT'S ON...	WHAT TO WEAR...
Parties & birthdays:	
....	....
....	....
Days out & holidays:	....
....	....
....	....
Other events:	....
....	....
....	....

Don't forget your SHOES!

Describe your BEST look of the month here

MY LOOK IS... ....

....

THE BEST BIT IS... ....

....

I WORE IT/WILL WEAR IT... ....

....

I BOUGHT IT/WILL BUY IT FROM... ....

....

THIS OUTFIT IS PERFECT FOR... HANGING OUT ☐ **PARTIES**  **SHOPPING** 

Add a stylish ring to go with your look.

Design a scarf to go with your look.

Don't forget the finishing touches to give your look the real wow factor!

What bag would look best with your outfit?

....

....

What colour shoes would you pick for your look?

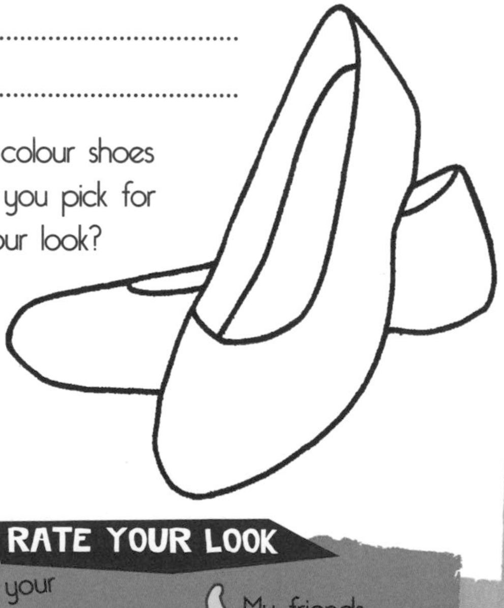

RATE YOUR LOOK

Give your outfit a score

/10

My friends

my look

DID YOU KNOW?

The average fashion show is only about ten minutes long.

GET THE LOOK

Whose look do you like this month? Stick or draw their pictures here.

STYLE SECRET

When opting for tight on top, go for loose on the bottom and vice versa.

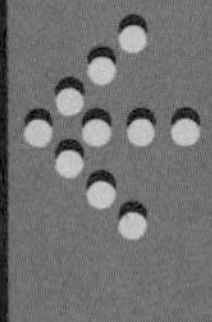

STEAL THE STYLE

FLORAL FASHION

From retro to exotic – find out the most stylish ways to wear florals, whatever the occasion.

WEAR IT WELL...

Get the look with some flowery fashion tips and tricks.

1 **Loud floral prints look great with neutral colours, so accessorize your look with a brown, black or white belt and shoes.**

2 **Just one floral accessory is enough to brighten up any outfit. Try a flowery scarf or bag to bring out your inner bloom.**

3 **Create a boho look by layering denim over your flowery print.**

4 **Avoid wearing the same floral pattern on the top and the bottom (unless it's a dress). Team a flowery skirt with a plain t-shirt or go for a print double-up and wear with another floral print.**

5 **Try a pair of floral shorts for a casual style or dress up for a special occasion with a bold-patterned dress.**

6 **Put a spring in your step with flower-print shoes.**

PERFECT PATTERN

With so many types of floral prints to choose from, it's important to choose a pattern that suits your taste and style, from dainty and delicate to big and bold. For a sophisticated look, opt for a smaller print, but if you want to stand out big is best.

Design your own floral pattern here.

FLOWER HAIR ACCESSORIES

Add some flower power to your look with some hair accessories to suit every hair style.

SHORT HAIR

★ flower slide
★ headband

MID LENGTH

★ flower behind the ear
★ hair garland

LONGER HAIR

★ flower coils in a plait
★ flowery hair bands

Turn to PAGE 20 to find out how to make your own hair accessories.

BLOOMING SPARKLES

A quick and easy way to get the look is to accessorize with some flowery jewellery. Look pretty as a picture with a single bloom cocktail ring, stud flower earrings or a statement flower bracelet.

NAIL THE STYLE

Paint your nails in pretty flowery shades, like pastel pink and lilac, or bold orange and red. Finish off with a cute flower nail sticker.

DID YOU KNOW?

One of the most famous floral fabrics is chintz. It was created in India around 1600 and exported all around the world, starting a global floral fashion trend that is still popular today.

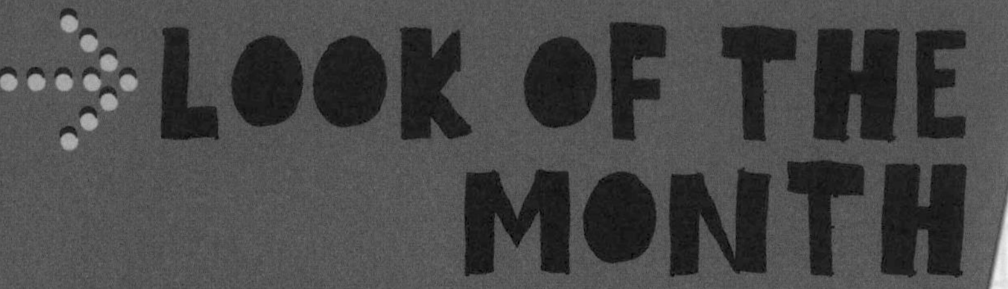

LOOK OF THE MONTH

MONTH..

Stick, draw or stencil a picture of your BEST outfit here

FASHION FORECAST

Plan your outfits for the month here...

WHAT'S ON...

Parties & birthdays:

....

....

Days out & holidays:

....

....

Other events:

....

....

WHAT TO WEAR...

....

....

....

....

....

....

....

....

Don't forget your SHOES!

Describe your BEST look of the month here

MY LOOK IS... ....

....

THE BEST BIT IS... ....

....

I WORE IT/WILL WEAR IT... ....

....

I BOUGHT IT/WILL BUY IT FROM... ....

....

THIS OUTFIT IS PERFECT FOR... HANGING OUT ☐ **PARTIES**  **SHOPPING** ☐

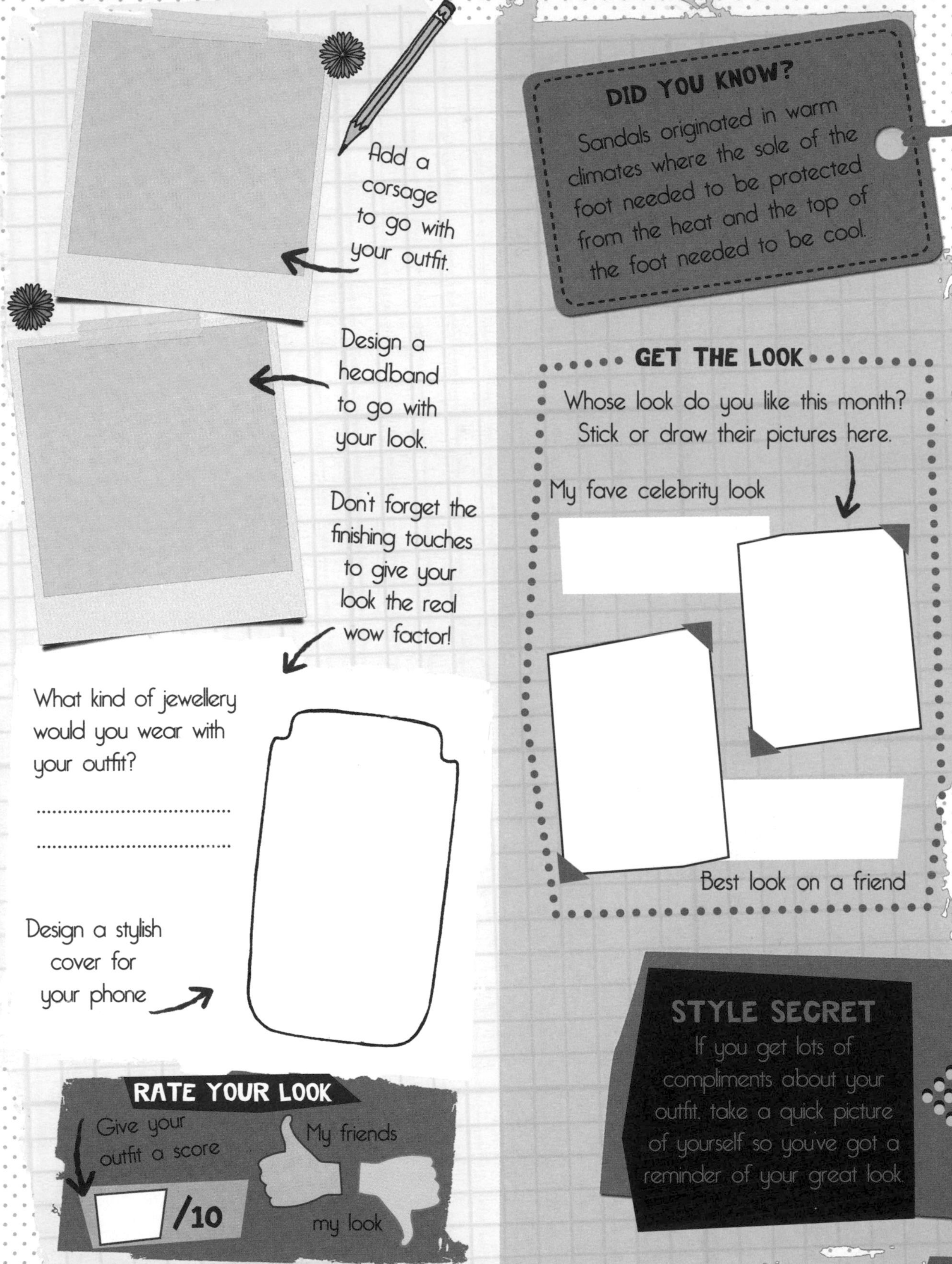
Add a corsage to go with your outfit.
Design a headband to go with your look.
Don't forget the finishing touches to give your look the real wow factor!
What kind of jewellery would you wear with your outfit?
Design a stylish cover for your phone
RATE YOUR LOOK
Give your outfit a score
/10
My friends
my look
DID YOU KNOW?
Sandals originated in warm climates where the sole of the foot needed to be protected from the heat and the top of the foot needed to be cool.
GET THE LOOK
Whose look do you like this month? Stick or draw their pictures here.
My fave celebrity look
Best look on a friend
STYLE SECRET
If you get lots of compliments about your outfit, take a quick picture of yourself so you've got a reminder of your great look.

STEAL THE STYLE

RED CARPET

You don't have to be a celebrity to dress like a star.

WEAR IT WELL...

Get the A-list look in five easy steps

1 Rule number one – it's all about the dress. Find one that can be worn lots of times and can be made to look like a new outfit every time, by teaming it with different accessories like a colourful jacket, belt or shoes.

2 Nothing will ruin your look more than the wrong bag. Keep it small and simple, just make sure there's enough room for a camera to get some shots of how great you look.

3 Stilettos are an instant way to add glamour, but wobbling around is not a good look, so opt for wedges if you need a more stable option.

4 You'll be tempted to pile on the bling, but for true star style, opt for just one statement piece like an eye-catching necklace or sparkly, dangly earrings.

5 Mix a bit of shimmery powder into your moisturizer to give yourself an all-over glow.

HAIR FLAIR

Make sure your hair is looking its very best with these glamorous styles.

1 A polished ponytail is a great style for making sure your hair looks neat for the whole of your event.

2 If your hair is normally straight, go for the wow factor with some glam Hollywood waves.

★ Take a section of hair and holding your curling iron in an upright position, curl the hair around it. Add a bit of hairspray to keep it in place.

★ Once you've curled all your hair, take a flat brush and gently brush out the curls to create your waves.

DO! Check what your friends are wearing to your big event to avoid turning up in the same outfit.

DRESS TO IMPRESS

With so many to choose from, picking the right dress can be tricky. Find out more about the different shapes and styles and tick which one you like best.

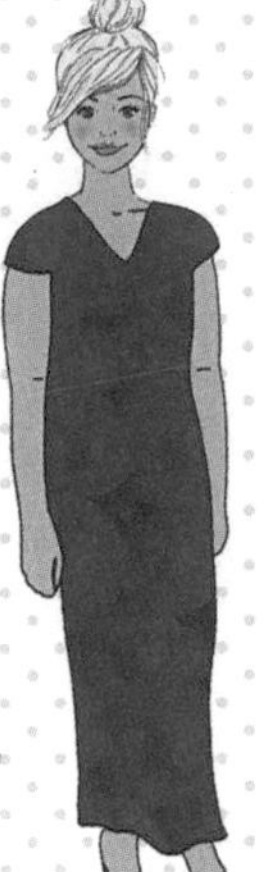

A column dress falls in a straight line and looks especially good if you're tall.

A ball gown has a tight-fitting bodice and the dramatic full skirt will make you feel (and look) like a princess.

An empire style has a high waistline that creates a long lean look and is comfortable to wear.

A short and sweet prom dress is perfect for parties and dancing around with your friends.

JEWELS RULE

Jewellery is a key part of this look and if you're wearing a dress, a necklace is a must have. Use this guide to help you work out the right necklace to wear, whatever your dress style.

SWEET-HEART NECKLINE
princess

HALTER NECK
princess or matinee

Draw in the right necklace for each of these dress styles.

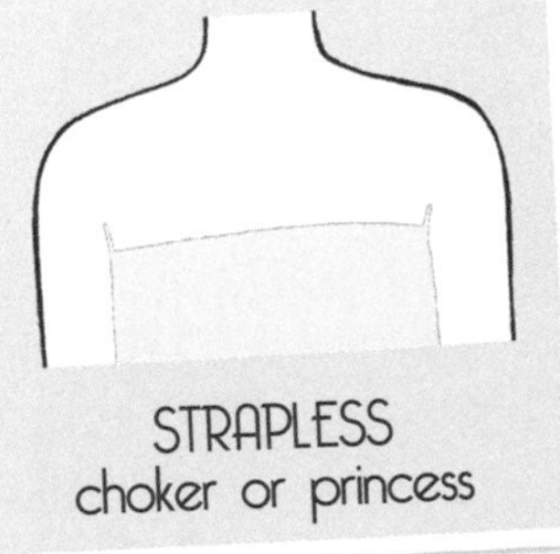

STRAPLESS
choker or princess

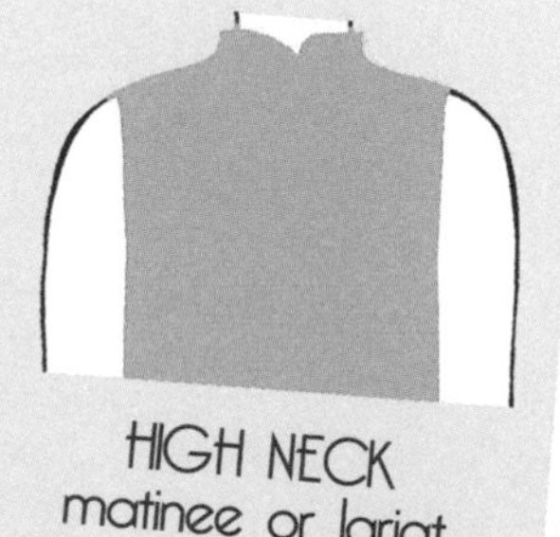

HIGH NECK
matinee or lariat

Make it!

TRANSFORM A CARDIGAN

Take one boring old cardigan and inject some fun!

1 **TOOLS:** cardigan, needle, thread, scissors, buttons **TIME:** 30 mins
SKILL LEVEL: ✂✂

For an instant update to an old cardigan simply change the buttons.

★ Snip off the old buttons and pick out any loose threads. Choose some new buttons to replace the old – you could opt for matching ones, lots of different ones, or your cardboard buttons for a unique look.

★ To attach your buttons, take a threaded needle and sew a couple of stitches in your cardigan, where you want to attach the buttons, before sewing several stitches through each button's holes.

★ Make sure you don't sew the buttons on too tightly to the cardigan fabric.

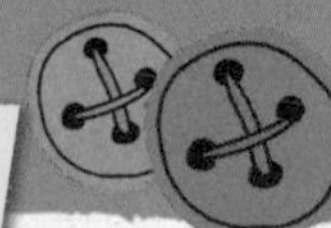

2 **TOOLS:** cardigan, sewing kit, scissors, tape measure, thick lace trim 1 to 2 metres **TIME:** 45 mins
SKILL LEVEL: ✂✂

Add some pretty lace to your cardigan for an on-trend update.

★ Measure around the bottom of your cardigan, add 5 cm and cut a length of thick lace to size.

★ Turn your cardigan inside out and pin the length of thick lace to the bottom of the cardigan, so it has a 2 cm overlap.

★ Sew the lace in place and turn the cardigan back the right way to wear.

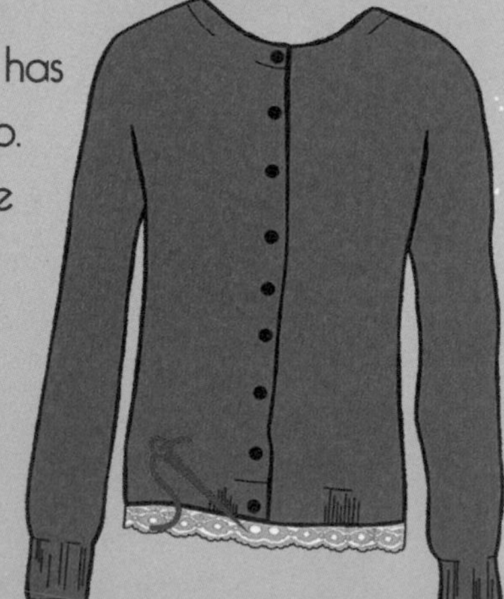

3 TOOLS: cardigan, measuring tape, scissors, needle, thread, belt

TIME: 20 mins **SKILL LEVEL:** ✂✂

Transform your cardigan from winter wear to a summer essential in minutes.

★ Turn your cardigan inside out and lay it on a flat surface. Cut between 10 cm and 20 cm off the length of one sleeve (depending on how short you want your sleeves to be). Turn the edge of the sleeve over and pin in place. Sew along the pins to finish the edge neatly.

★ Do the same for the other sleeve, making sure it is cut and turned back to the same length. Then turn the cardigan back the right way and wear with a colourful belt to brighten it up.

DID YOU KNOW?
The cardigan got its name from the 7th Earl of Cardigan, who was known for wearing open-fronted jumpers in the Crimean War in 1853.

3 ways to wear your CARDIGAN

1 Layer your cardigan over a hoodie, for a casual but cool style.

2 Tuck your cardigan into a skirt (or a belt) to give your outfit a stylish edge.

3 Sling your cardigan over your shoulders and team with a stripy t-shirt to create a nautical look.

FASHION FAVOURITES

It's official – you are a true fashionista and style specialist.

What's been your best look of the year? Draw it here.

Don't forget your SHOES!

If you could only pass on one style secret to your friends, what would it be?

....

....

....

....

....

What were your top three makes?

1 ....

....

2 ....

....

3 ....

....

BEST TREND

Tick which style trends you looked best in.

- DENIM ☐
- ANIMAL PRINT ☐
- SPORTS STAR ☐
- BEACH BABE ☐
- WINTER ☐
- FESTIVAL CHIC ☐
- PARTY TIME ☐
- NAUTICAL STYLE ☐
- ROCK CHICK ☐
- BRIGHT & BOLD ☐
- FLORAL FASHION ☐
- RED CARPET ☐

DON'T FORGET TO

★ Stay on trend by keeping up with the latest fashion news.

★ Develop your style by experimenting with new looks.

★ Create outfits you look and feel fabulous in and you'll always be a fashion winner.

TECHNICAL TERMS

A-LINE The style of clothing where a skirt or dress is fitted at the hips and gradually widens towards the hem, following the shape of a capital letter A.

APPLIQUE Needlework where pieces of fabric or gems are stuck onto a larger piece to form a picture or a pattern.

BANDEAU A strapless style of top or dress.

BODYCON A tight, formfitting style of clothing.

COLUMN A slim-fitting style of dress with a straight, narrow shape. Also known as sheath.

COMPLEMENTARY COLOURS Colours that are opposite each other on the colour wheel. Red and green are complementary colours.

EMPIRE LINE The style of clothing where the waistline is cut just under the bust and the rest of the dress is loosely fitted.

MAXI A casual, usually sleevless dress that falls to the ankles.

PEPLUM A short strip of fabric attached the waist of a jacket, dress or blouse to create a hanging frill.

RETRO Clothing made to look like styles from the past.

SHIFT A short, simple, sleevless dress that hangs loosely from the shoulders.

VINTAGE Clothing made between 1920-1960.

THIS IS A CARLTON BOOK

First pubished in 2019 by Carlton Books Limited
An imprint of the Carlton Publishing Group
20 Mortimer Street,
London, WIT 3JW

A catalogue record for this book is available from the British Library.

9 8 7 6 5 4 3 2 1
ISBN: 978-1-78312-501-2
Printed and bound in Dubai

Author: Caroline Rowlands
Illustrator: Sam Loman